Unwin Education Books: 24

CREATIVE TEACHING

Unwin Education Books

Series Editor: Ivor Morrish, B.D., B.A., Dip.Ed. (London), B.A. (Bristol)

Unwin Education Books: 24
Series Editor: Ivor Morrish

Creative Teaching

An Approach to the Achievement of Educational Objectives

S. HOWARD NICHOLLS
M.Ed., D.C.P.
Lecturer in Education, The Queen's University of Belfast

AUDREY NICHOLLS
M.Ed., Dip.Ed.Psych.
Director of Studies and Head of the Department of Home Economics, The Northern Ireland Polytechnic

London
GEORGE ALLEN & UNWIN LTD
RUSKIN HOUSE   MUSEUM STREET

First published in 1975

ISBN 0 04 371039 5   hardback
       0 04 371040 9   paperback

0035042.

Printed in Great Britain
in 10/11 point Times Roman type
by The Devonshire Press Ltd
Barton Road, Torquay Devon

To Our Parents

Acknowledgements

We are very grateful to Frank and Marjorie Jackson who made many helpful comments on the manuscript, and to Eileen Baines who typed it.

Contents

Chapter 1

The Nature of the Problem

Education, like the society of which it is such a vital and integral part, has undergone many changes in recent years and, indeed, is continuing to change. Teachers and, more particularly, head teachers in this country still exercise considerable influence and control over education and since teachers differ considerably in their atttitudes to change, the extent to which changes have taken place and the nature of these changes vary throughout the country. Teacher control and influence over curriculum matters affect not only the rate at which any changes might take place but also largely determine the nature of the curriculum and result in tremendous variations in different schools. Teachers are not the only influence on educational change: national and local authority decisions frequently have considerable effect in bringing it about. Although decisions of this kind are often reached after consultations with teachers or with teacher participation, they affect teachers as a whole, many of whom are not directly involved in the decision-making. Other influences on change such as teachers' centres, local advisers, HMIs, in-service courses, national figures and educational literature, usually have their effect more directly on individual teachers.

To an observer of our educational system the picture of change probably appears to be confused and yet it is possible to indentify some general trends which have emerged or are emerging. A major trend is that of greater concern with and interest in education. Parents, employers, the press and the general public as well as the students themselves now tend to take a lively and often well-informed interest in education. They also show a serious concern with its quality, its form and its purposes. The practical aspects of this greater interest show themselves in the increasing numbers of pupils who continue their education beyond the statutory leaving age and the increasing numbers receiving further education and studying for qualifications of all kinds. Less obvious, and far more difficult to assess, is the influence of students, parents, employers and the press on what is included in the curriculum. Increasingly students state their views on what and how they should be taught and sometimes use more active ways of showing their dissatisfaction. Pressure groups of parents are heard more frequently expressing their views on education. Critical and constructive articles on education appear increasingly in the press. While some of the comments and observations from these various sources might be ill-informed, others show considerable insight into educational matters. The extent to which these influences are actually reflected in curricula is hard to assess, but there can be little doubt that they reflect widespread interest.

Along with this greater interest in education is a concern that there should be equality of educational opportunity for all. Translated into practical terms, this concern has led, among other things, to a widespread abolition of selection of pupils at the end of the primary stage and to a considerable reorganisation of secondary education along comprehensive lines. With the realisation that in many comprehensive schools the selection that had not taken place at the primary stage was being carried out at the secondary stage, a slight but clearly discernible trend is now emerging, namely a call for the abolition of streaming within comprehensive schools. To stream or not to stream has long been an issue, both in primary and secondary schools, but within comprehensive systems it raises further considerations.

Concern for equality of educational opportunity has also led to positive discrimination being made in an attempt to compensate for social deprivation. Several major researches had suggested the existence of a relationship between educational attainment and social and cultural background, but it was the Plowden Report that advocated forms of positive discrimination in favour of primary schools in which there are many socially deprived pupils.

In some quarters a trend has emerged of genuine and positive attempts to include in the education process more than just the acquisition of a body of knowledge which is to be remembered and regurgitated in examinations. These attempts manifest themselves in a variety of ways. In some instances there is a concern for the development of a wide range of intellectual abilities such as the ability to detect fallacies in arguments, the ability to relate cause and effect, the ability to present a logical argument, the ability to separate the relevant from the irrelevant. In addition, there is a positive concern for the inclusion of social and emotional objectives. Objectives such as these have been stated by teachers for a long time but *on the whole* it has been largely a question of merely paying lip-service to them. In the case of the development of intellectual skills, it was frequently assumed that these are an automatic by-product of learning academic subjects, while in the case of emotional and social objectives the assumption was that these were achieved *automatically* through the house-system, out-of-school activities and the general 'ethos' of the school, or simply by exhortation. The current trend is for positive attempts to be made to include learning opportunities for the achievement of these objectives in the curriculum (which includes 'out-of-school activities'), rather than simply leave them to chance.

There is also an increased concern for each individual child. The concern is very real, both at the primary and secondary levels, and a great deal is said and written about inter- and intra-pupil differences. To provide for individuals in the curriculum is very difficult and makes great demands on teachers. At the practical level, moves have been made towards individualising learning, perhaps more so at the primary than at the secondary level, but we still have a long way to go in this direction.

The above general trends are reflected in the curriculum: in what is taught and learned, in approaches to learning, in forms of school and pupil organisation, in pupil-teacher relationships and in methods of examining and forms of assessment. A wider range of subjects is now taught. In both primary and secondary schools teachers are experimenting with a variety of approaches to learning instead of relying on a particular and favoured approach, and are using a wider range of ancillary aids. In many schools pupils might be seen working by themselves on occasions, at other times working in groups of varying sizes and sometimes as a whole class. Links have been established with the community, two-way links so that pupils go out into the community and use its various resources in a variety of ways, and parents and other visitors come into the school for a variety of purposes. It is not unknown for parents to be seen working with their own children when attempts are being made to link more closely the home and the school.

Such a brief sketch of some of the present trends in education as they appear to the writers can do no more than to indicate the range and variety of changes and developments and illustrate the point that current educational change is complex and widespread and has many forms. In a situation in which education is seeking to further a wider variety of objectives in a multiplicity of ways and in which education is open to a wider range of social influence and in which change is proceeding at a greatly increased speed, teachers are faced with more complex and fluid conditions than those which existed only twenty or thirty years ago. It is not surprising, therefore, to find in such circumstances that some curriculum changes appear to have been made in a haphazard and piecemeal fashion and without any rational basis. The basic idea which runs through this book is that educational change is more likely to be effective and justifiable when it is carefully planned with clear and reasonable purposes in mind and when the curricula thus devised reflect what is practically possible and not just theoretically desirable.

There are a number of ways of planning the whole or part of a curriculum, each way having its own strengths and weaknesses, as well as its own advocates. One procedure, described by the writers elsewhere[1] and outlined briefly by the Schools Council[2] is sometimes described as an 'objectives approach'. (A similar approach is also advocated by many other writers such as Saylor and Alexander (1966), Taba (1971), Tyler (1969) and Wheeler (1967).[3])

This procedure is rational and logical and requires a rigorous application of knowledge from the major educational disciplines. In essence the procedure favoured by the writers calls for the detailed analysis of one's actual teaching situation, the selection of objectives, the selection and organisation of content and methods thought likely to achieve the objectives, and the assessment of the extent to which the objectives have been achieved, followed by feedback of knowledge and experience to improve or modify the curriculum—so that the procedure becomes cyclical in nature. Stated simply and somewhat starkly in this way, this approach to curriculum development appears to be acceptable to teachers. However, further analysis and more detailed discussion of the process frequently reveal opposition from some teachers, so that although the approach has some following in this country it has not yet been adopted on a widespread scale by practising teachers. Some of the possible reasons for this state of affairs will be examined in the next chapter.

One of the major purposes of this book is to make a close and detailed examination of certain aspects of the approach to curriculum planning that has just been briefly outlined. In particular this will be concerned with the many and varied considerations to be taken into account in the creation of learning opportunities to achieve stated objectives. It is hoped to show how objectives can be used to give greater clarity and objectivity to curriculum planning without imposing undue restrictions on teacher initiative and freedom. Other aspects of curriculum planning to be studied include assessment and evaluation, record keeping and the implementation of new approaches.

Several general points about an 'objectives approach' to curriculum planning might usefully close this introductory chapter. Such an approach lends itself well to, and indeed is probably most effectively operated by, co-operative effort by groups of teachers. When teachers come together to undertake curriculum planning using this framework, certain advantages may accrue, over and above the new curriculum itself.[4] It is quite likely that many ideas which were vague and unclear will become clearer. Vagueness in thinking and the consequent loose use of words causes much confusion and many difficulties in education. A rigorous approach to curriculum development, based on a logical framework, can do much to overcome this and can lead to clearer thinking and more precise use of educational terms.

Moreover, by going back to fundamental principles and by asking (and answering) searching and difficult questions about what they are trying to achieve, teachers frequently find themselves involved in real rather than superficial curriculum change. If thinking and discussion of this nature take place during curriculum planning not only is the curriculum more likely to prove effective, but the planning activities can provide a most valuable form of in-service education, which is at the same time of both an intellectual and practical kind.

However, it should not be thought that such advantages are automatic by-products of this approach to curriculum planning; they can only occur under certain circumstances. A most important factor is the quality of leadership available, whether this is embodied in a formal leader or distributed more informally among group members. The leadership should be knowledgeable and skilful in a variety of matters including the particular approach to curriculum development being used, the relevant disciplines of education, group dynamics, organisation and administration, resource materials and assessment techniques, and also should have personal qualities which will enable group members to accept the leadership offered. In addition, the leadership should be aware of the potential benefits of using this approach and have the skill to enable group members to derive these benefits.

Time is a vital factor in curriculum planning. If it is to be carried out properly and if the kind of advantages mentioned above are hoped for, then adequate time has to be made available. This is not to suggest that there should be no time-limit or that dead-lines should not be set. Indeed, these are important as a means of keeping work moving, but they should be realistic and should allow time for full discussion and thought, especially if attitudes are to be changed. The time factor can be a very real practical problem if all or part of a school staff are working together. Too often curriculum planning has to be carried out in hurried sessions during lunch times or after school. This might be one reason why comparatively little real curriculum *innovation* has its origin in the school. Teachers frequently take innovations originating outside the school and adapt these, just as they adapt or modify existing school courses and practice. These activities are less demanding in terms of time but not necessarily so in terms of knowledge and expertise.

There are other factors which are important to any approach to curriculum development: money, material resources, administrative support, adequate manpower, to mention but a few. It is suggested, however, important as these are, that skilled leadership and adequate time are absolutely fundamental to the approach described here.

NOTES

1 A. and H. Nicholls, *Developing a Curriculum* (Allen & Unwin, 1972).
2 Schools Council Working Paper No. 10, *Curriculum Development: Teachers' Groups and Centres* (HMSO, 1967).
3 J. G. Saylor and W. M. Alexander, *Curriculum Planning for Modern Schools* (Holt, Rinehart & Winston, 1966); H. Taba, *Curriculum Development: Theory and Practice* (Harcourt, Brace & World, 1971); R. W. Tyler, *Basic Principles of Curriculum and Instruction* (University of Chicago Press, 1969); D. K. Wheeler, *Curriculum Process* (University of London Press, 1967).
4 See also Nicholls, op. cit., and Taba, op. cit.

Chapter 2

An Approach
through Objectives

The approach to curriculum planning outlined briefly in the previous chapter is not widely practised by teachers in this country, partly because of lack of familiarity and partly because of lack of sympathy with it. Increasingly, however, newly-qualified teachers are entering the profession having studied this and other approaches to curriculum development, while in-service courses are making good the lack of familiarity on the part of serving teachers. The problem of unfamiliarity, therefore, is likely to decrease but the problem of lack of sympathy with or, in some cases, downright opposition to the structured approach of the ends-means model remains a serious and fundamental one.

Most of the arguments raised against this model are centred on the specification of objectives. The arguments tend to fall into two main categories: those which reject the whole idea of specifying objectives in advance of teaching-learning activities and those which criticise the stating of objectives in behavioural terms. Proponents of the former type of argument are likely to believe that a teacher cannot possibly know the whole range of responses which pupils might make in a learning situation and that to state objectives and to work towards these is restricting pupils' growth. There are several implications which may be inherent in this belief. One is that it is the pupils who decide what they will learn and that the teacher's responsibility is simply to present the stimulus or learning material. This is a perfectly tenable viewpoint but one wonders whether all teachers who take up this position actually permit in the classroom the variety of individual responses they talk about and whether they encourage pupil participation in planning what is to be learned. If they do not, and instead guide or direct their pupils along certain lines of their (the teacher's) choosing and/or reward particular behaviours then, whether they recognise it or not, they are working towards certain predetermined objectives. In selecting what to teach and how to teach it in the first place, they are pursuing certain objectives, albeit unstated ones, as they also do when they select certain pupil responses and reward these in preference to others. Of course, most teachers do have objectives in mind for their pupils, but those who argue against stating them in advance seem to concentrate on what they as teachers are going to do without considering what their actions are intended to achieve. It is a fact that all the possible objectives which pupils might achieve are unlikely to be known in advance, but surely some are known and considered desirable and these can be stated. Stating some does not preclude the achievement of others, but rather increases the possibility of achieving those that are stated. Moreover, few people involved in curriculum development work would suggest that a set of objectives should remain static; new ones can be added and existing ones can be changed or even omitted, should evidence from the classroom suggest that such actions are necessary.

Another group of arguments is directed not so much against the pre-specification of objectives but rather against the specificity with which objectives are stated. Expressions such as 'the engineering model' and 'management by objectives' are used to describe the objectives approach, with comments or overtones indicating or implying that such an approach is undesirable in education which is concerned with the development of young human beings. In rejecting the notion of stating objectives in behavioural terms, some critics reject totally the notion of an ends-means model, for quite different reasons than those mentioned above.

Some of these critics are not against the idea of making general statements of intent, statements that are usually called aims, but they are against making precise statements of the expected changes in pupil behaviour as a result of particular educational activities, in other words, in terms of behavioural objectives. Again, a number of reasons are given to support this viewpoint. Some teachers feel that the approach is too restricting, that stating objectives with clarity and precision makes the teaching-learning situation inflexible and too tightly controlled. It is also claimed that only trivial behaviours can be expressed clearly and precisely and so important aspects of education are neglected by this approach. A further argument is that it is simply not possible in some areas of the curriculum to express one's intentions in behavioural terms.[1]

It is our view that objectives can be stated at various levels of specificity and be of value in curriculum planning and assessment, and that the ends-means model can be usefully adopted by teachers with widely differing views about the nature of objectives. We will offer some example objectives to illustrate this point of view.

As a general rule, few teachers would be happy to state *all* their objectives with such precision and specificity as the following:

1. names the capital cities of six countries in Europe
2. adds together tens and units up to fifty with at least 90 per cent. success
3. identifies all the symbols on a weather map
4. lists in chronological order the battles in the Civil War

If all objectives were stated at this level of specificity, there would be so many that teachers would be unable to remember them all. Moreover, teaching and learning would tend to become exceedingly fragmented if it were based on objectives of this type and would tend to be concerned with rather low-level behaviours. There are occasions, however, when it is appropriate to state objectives in such a specific way. For example, if pupils were experiencing some difficulty in learning, then that which was to be learned might usefully be broken down into small steps, expressed in a series of specific and related objectives. The learning problem might arise from difficulty inherent in that to be learned, from some lack of ability on the part of the learners or from some handicap brought about by absence. Specific objectives are necessary if one is to develop some kinds of material for programmed learning. Indeed, some writers who advocate an extreme position with regard to behavioural objectives do so in terms of programmed learning.[2] Although few teachers would support this position for normal teaching purposes, the work of these writers has been most useful in encouraging us to think more clearly about statements of objectives. Moreover, by expressing objectives in terms of what the pupils are intended to do, attention is directed to the learner and away from the teacher and from what is to be learned.

At the other end of the objectives continuum we find statements such as these:

1. to develop good citizens
2. to encourage good social relationships
3. to foster an attitude of inquiry
4. to encourage an appreciation of the arts
5. to develop positive attitudes to work
6. to foster the all-round development of pupils.

These are statements of a most general kind which are usually called *aims.* Statements of this kind indicate a general direction and if we examine the form in which they are written we see that they are expressed in terms of what it is hoped the teacher or a particular course or indeed education in general might achieve. Compare these statements and their form with those above.

Few teachers would be opposed to making broad general statements of this kind to indicate their intentions, and statements of the kind just illustrated are likely to receive widespread support. Many teachers would consider the examples listed above desirable aims of education. However, these statements are quite vague and therefore permit a wide variety of interpretation. This is one reason why they receive widespread support: each teacher gives his own meaning to them.

If statements such as these are put forward as desirable aims towards which teachers should be directing their efforts, they need to be analysed to establish what is meant by them. Such analysis of the term used is likely to reveal differences of opinion. What do we mean, for example, by a good citizen? Is this the same thing to a teacher holding communist views as it is to one who is a right-wing conservative? If not, then the approaches to this aim as interpreted by those teachers would vary considerably. It is perfectly acceptable and even desirable that teachers use different approaches to achieve the same or similar aims and objectives, but attention is being drawn here to the problems or even dangers in using vague general statements which *apparently* receive widespread support and agreement, but which *in practice* mean very different things.

In terms of curriculum planning one must question the practical value of aims stated at this broad general level. Are they of any help at all in selecting and organising content, in selecting methods, in organising learning or in any of the *detailed* decisions which have to be made in planning a unit or course? The answer must be in the negative. Before they can be of use in guiding such detailed decisions the broad general statements have to be restated or interpreted in more precise terms. A number of questions have to be asked. What do we mean by a good citizen? What would pupils be doing if they were displaying the qualities of a good citizen? With which aspects of pupils' development are we concerned? Are they all of equal importance? What do we mean by the arts? What are pupils doing when they show appreciation? What are positive attitudes to work? Shall we be satisfied if these are shown only when we are supervising or should they be displayed when we are elsewhere in the room or school? What do we mean by good social relationships? Are we concerned with pupil-pupil relationships, pupil-teacher or pupil-community, or all of these? These are difficult questions for a group of teachers to answer, but answers are necessary before one can proceed to plan a curriculum on the basis of aims of this nature.

It might be asked, then, whether aims of this kind serve any useful purpose at all. It is not an uncommon situation for fine-sounding aims to be put proudly at the beginning of a course or in a head teacher's statement about the school and then to be forgotten until speech day or an inspector's visit to the school. In such circumstances they serve little useful purpose. However, if they are treated seriously they can provide a useful *starting point* for thinking about curriculum planning and can indicate an orientation which the curriculum might take. A statement of several aims can give an indication of balance in the curriculum. It can be examined for any possible omissions or undue and unwanted emphases. It also offers the opportunity to make decisions about priorities so that, if necessary, a hierarchical order can be established. Such a statement also provides a base on which broad general decisions can be made of the kind outlined in Chapter 5.

We have examined what might be regarded as the extreme positions of the objectives continuum and the point has been made that one position is unlikely to commend itself to many teachers for general use and that the other is useful largely as a starting point but of little value in the practicalities of detailed decision-making in curriculum planning. Between these two extremes are a number of positions which can be taken; the position which a teacher may choose to take can depend on a number of factors: the teacher's own view of education, the particular situation in which he finds himself or the nature of what is to be learned.

Some teachers fear that by using an objectives approach, considerable restraints are being put on their actions and that much teacher freedom is in danger of being eroded. It must be stated that if a teacher is working towards a set of pre-stated objectives certain restraints are indeed imposed upon him. These restraints require that classroom activities are directed towards the objectives. However, if the teacher has selected or helped to select the objectives there is no serious diminution in his freedom and in his control over the curriculum.

Objectives stated at a more general level allow more freedom to the teacher than those stated more precisely, as may be seen by examining two examples. If an objective is for pupils to 'name the symbols on a given weather map', different teachers may use different approaches for its achievement or the same teacher may use different approaches with different pupils, but what is to be learned is stated quite clearly for both teacher and pupil. There is a known *minimum* of what is to be learned. On the other hand, if an objective is for pupils to 'construct animal figures using a wide variety of materials', the limits are less restricted. A wide variety of materials could be offered by the teacher, each teacher being at liberty to select his own range, as well as allowing pupils the opportunity to make a choice from what is available or to find alternative materials. The objective also permits the pupils to choose any animal figures and to interpret the construction of them in their own way.

These two examples are taken from quite different areas of the curriculum and it might be the case that the same teacher would consider it appropriate to state objectives quite precisely and impose a fairly restricted limit in geography while stating objectives less precisely and allowing greater freedom in the creative arts. The difference here may lie in the differing nature of the subject matter; what is considered to be appropriate for one area of the curriculum might not be so for another.

However, even within the same area of the curriculum teachers may choose to state their objectives at varying levels of specificity for different reasons. Consider the following objectives:

1. reads books for pleasure during library periods
2. reads at least three of the following books during library periods:

Oliver Twist	*David Copperfield*
Little Women	*Treasure Island*
Black Beauty	*Kidnapped*
The Just-So Stories	*Peter Pan*
Gulliver's Travels	*Robinson Crusoe.*

The first objective implies a large element of choice on the part of the pupils with the teacher acting as an adviser and consultant. It also emphasises the pleasure aspect of reading. The two factors taken together might reflect a certain view of education, namely that pupils should be encouraged to make choices and that enjoyment is an important aspect of education. Or, they might indicate that the pupils for whom this objective is intended have not been in the habit of exercising choice and that they also do not find reading enjoyable and need to be helped and encouraged to derive pleasure from it. The objective might indicate both the above factors, or indeed others.

The second objective implies a more structured situation. There is an element of choice but this is within a restricted range decided by the teacher and there is no reference to the pleasure aspect. This again may reflect a certain view of education, in this case that pupils should make choices only within limits set by the teacher and that there are certain things which pupils should do in schools (like reading books thought of as children's classics). It might indicate, however, that the pupils for whom the objective is intended, need or want considerable guidance in choosing reading books. Neither objective should be considered right or wrong or better or worse in isolation. The two examples show that the level of specificity at which objectives are expressed can be a fairly complex matter and may be dependent on a number of factors.

We have tried to show how objectives can be stated at varying levels of specificity to allow for different circumstances and for teachers' differing views of education in an attempt to suggest that the ends-means model of curriculum planning need not be linked exclusively with the notion of ends being stated in precise behavioural terms. It is hoped that this may encourage those teachers who are unsympathetic to the notion of behavioural objectives to consider in a new light this particular approach to curriculum development. Most teachers would be happy with a level of specificity which gives suffi- cient guidance for planning and teaching but which does not direct or restrict them too much.

Another group of teachers who may favour this way of planning curricula are those who wish to offer a wide variety of approaches to cater for individual differences, and who fear that this method may result in a standardisation of learning opportunities. This *can* result, just as it can from any other way of curriculum planning but it is certainly not a particular feature of this method. There are two import- ant factors to be borne in mind. The first is that there are many ways of achieving the same objectives, so that a teacher wishing to provide for some individual differences can do so by offering a wide variety of routes to the same ends. Another teacher, not wishing to provide such a degree of flexibility, can, of course, use a different route, when one route has failed, or consolidate what has been learned or simply offer a change.

If a teacher wishes his pupils to achieve the objective 'understands the circulatory system', he could provide several ways for his pupils to achieve this. These might include listening to a talk based on a chart, watching a filmstrip and a moving sound film, dissecting a rabbit, reading an illustrated chapter in a textbook and using a programmed text. Any combination of these could be used by individuals or by the whole class, or individuals could select preferred ways of learning from those available.

The second factor to be taken into account is that a teacher can have different objectives for different pupils. In such a situation it may be that there is a basic core of objectives for all pupils and then over and above these are others for individual pupils according to their various and particular needs and abilities, or it may be that the teacher has a different set of objectives for each pupil. Both these circumstances would result in a highly complex organisation of learning opportunities which would make great demands on the teacher. Nevertheless, they are circumstances within which some teachers choose to operate.

The example objectives given so far in this chapter have been single unrelated statements, quoted to illustrate certain points. In reality, however, the situation is more complex because teachers are usually working towards a set of objectives, some of which, at various times according to particular circumstances, are likely to have greater priority than others. A set of objectives provides the possibility of a wide variety of approaches and of a range of interrelationships among the learning opportunities provided for its achievement. Sometimes a set of objectives will include objectives that are related to a particular subject or topic and others which have been agreed by the whole staff and can be pursued through all or several areas of the curriculum and/ or are relevant for pupils at all or several stages of education. The latter type are sometimes referred to as over-arching objectives.

A set of objectives for part of a social studies course might be as follows:

1. summarises the functions of the town council
2. states how a local election works
3. describes a council meeting
4. explains how the rates are used
5. works co-operatively with other pupils
6. works independently without supervision.

Objectives 1 to 4 are specific to the social studies course while object- ives 5 and 6 are over-arching objectives to be pursued throughout the curriculum wherever and whenever possible.

In planning learning opportunities for the achievement of these objectives, the set should be studied as a whole and the possible inter- relationships examined. Objective 5 suggests that opportunities should be provided for some forms of group work, while objective 6 indicates that pupils will be working without constant supervision of their teacher and on their own initiative. Taken with objective 3, objective 5 and/or 6 could suggest an opportunity in which pupils visit a council meeting either on their own initiative or following the teacher's arrangements. Pupils might work together to stage a mock election in pursuit of objectives 2 and 5. Individual or group research in reference libraries or interviews with local officials and councillors could be undertaken in pursuit of all or combinations of the objectives. Groups of varying size and composition could be used. It might be considered necessary by the teacher to emphasise objective 5 for some pupils and objective 6 for others, depending on their particular needs. For many pupils, more opportunities than those just indicated might have to be provided before they made satisfactory progress towards the objectives.

A set of objectives such as this does not necessarily indicate one particular approach, nor does it indicate that the same approach must be used for all pupils, but it often suggests a type of approach, as the above example illustrates. A statement of objectives does not constitute a straitjacket for teachers or pupils. Rather, it provides a framework to guide other curriculum decisions and a focus towards which teacher and pupils can direct their efforts.

The possibility of conflict among the interested parties is an important issue when stating objectives. Conflict might be about their importance, about inclusions or omissions or about priorities. If there is to be conflict, it will exist whether objectives are explicitly stated or merely implied. Stating objectives explicitly brings the conflict right out into the open and provides the opportunity for it to be recognised and discussed and perhaps resolved.

Conflict about objectives might exist among various combinations of people concerned with the curriculum. It might exist, for example, among members of staff in the same school. Some teachers might consider, for instance, that objectives concerned with pupils' responsibility for their own learning, pupils' independence, decision-making, research techniques and social development are of paramount importance, while other teachers in the same school give priority to the acquisition of a body of knowledge. It might be argued that variety in objectives, even in the same school, is to be desired rather than condemned as this will ensure that certain aspects of education are not neglected. Variety is indeed desirable and to be encouraged, but it should be seen as an appropriate balance among different aspects of pupil development and should be planned for, rather than allowed to emerge in a haphazard and uncontrolled way. Moreover, some objectives are difficult to achieve and may take several years of concerted effort on the part of many teachers before pupils show much evidence of progress towards them. Objectives of this type would include the cognitive and affective objectives illustrated in Chapter 6. Joint planning and co-operative efforts among staff are necessary for the successful achievement by most pupils of objectives such as these. Further, where there is direct and marked conflict among teachers' objectives, it is unlikely that pupils will show much development to-wards any of the conflicting objectives, thus much time and effort will be wasted, and it is possible that some pupils may experience distress in trying to cope with the conflicting demands.

It has been suggested that variety, in the form of a wide range of objectives and in a multiplicity of approaches to their achievement, is to be encouraged. If variety becomes conflict, difficulties for pupils may follow, which in turn may cause problems for teachers. Staff discussion of objectives will reveal areas of marked disagreement and difference. It might be possible for members of staff to arrive at a compromise position, or the head teacher may decide where the emphasis in objectives is to be, or he may be able, by careful plan-ning, to minimise the effects of the differing viewpoints. Whatever the solution in a particular school, it is surely preferable that conflict of this kind should be recognised and brought out into the open, and action taken to reduce any undesired effects.

Even in schools where there is general agreement about objectives among staff, conflict may arise from other sources. Objectives which teachers consider to be important and are actively pursuing with their pupils may be at variance with what is considered important in the society in which the pupils live and will work. For example, teachers may believe it to be very important that pupils should work together co-operatively, whereas in society the emphasis may be very strongly in terms of competitive work. Is the school to attempt to redress what society considers important or should the school be preparing its pupils to fit in with society? Teachers need to consider their objectives very seriously and to ask searching questions about what they are trying to do.

Similar questions need to be posed and answered when the school's objectives are at variance with those of its pupils and their parents. The Schools Council's *Enquiry I*[3] indicates that such variance is not uncommon. In some schools pupils' and parents' objectives are related directly to getting a job and other practical issues, while the objectives of many teachers are much wider than this and include cultural, leisure and character aspects of education. It is unlikely that such fundamental differences can be completely resolved, but perhaps some reconciliation can take place if teachers discuss their objectives with pupils and parents and justify their choice. At the same time teachers should acquaint themselves with the objectives which pupils and parents believe to be important and, at the very least, be prepared *to consider* including these with their own objectives.

The selection of an appropriate set of objectives is probably the most important stage in curriculum planning. It is an exercise which requires knowledge, skills, effort and time, but when carried out provides a rational base from which further curriculum decisions can be made. Without such a base curriculum decisions are likely to be made on the basis of whim, fancy, fashion, expediency or personal preference. These are hardly appropriate bases for members of a skilled profession to adopt.

NOTES

1 For a full account of arguments for and against the use of behavioural objectives see: W. J. Popham, Probing the Validity of Arguments against Behavioural Goals in *Current Research on Instruction,* R. C. Anderson *et al.* (eds) (Prentice Hall, 1969), pp. 66–72.

2 See particularly R. F. Mager, *Preparing Instructional Objectives* (Fearon, 1962).

3 Schools Council, *Enquiry 1: Young School Leavers* (HMSO, 1968).

Chapter 3

Social Factors

The process of learning is continuous and is influenced not only by innate potential and the physical circumstances in which a person lives, but also by other people. This is because others, directly or indirectly, purposely or innocently, exert their influence on the opportunities for learning that are available and on the behaviours they reward, ignore or punish.

The teacher seeks to influence learning but finds himself in the position of having the pupil for so short a period of time that much (and perhaps most) of a pupil's learning occurs outside the school. The teacher is also in the position of having that which is learned outside the school impinging on what he is trying to teach his pupil so that aims and objectives, the approach and the evaluation need to be created in such a way as to take this fact into account. For this reason, through knowledge of his pupils as social beings in contact with and learning from groups and individuals outside school, the teacher needs to sensitise himself to their individual and group needs.

Sensitivity to the needs of pupils can be rather difficult for a teacher at times, especially if he comes from a background that is very different from that of his pupils and if he has a superior intellectual competence and more helpful patterns of motivation. He may not see or feel why his pupils are not so keen on history as he was, or why they do not respond to his call for higher marks in their essays, or why they get no intellectual satisfaction from discussing the characters in a Shakespeare play. In such a case the teacher may be a prisoner of his own social background and schooling and of the idea that education is the passing on of what he learned, using the same approach as his own teachers, rather than a living, changing and creative concept. A danger of lack of knowledge and understanding lies in the possible lack of sympathy and patience a teacher has for a child who does not come up to his expectations.

Because of the importance of seeing the child as a social being as well as in terms of intellectual potential and intellectual accomplishments, the student teacher is often asked to carry out a child study and, prior to teaching practice, is encouraged to visit the school concerned and make notes on the children he will teach. In both cases he will note social factors, among other things, with the idea of using this knowledge when he designs the learning opportunities. Similar actions will be taken by teachers when they have a new class or go to a new school. Student teachers, however, often have more time to carry out their investigations than practising teachers and are often in the position of being able to make a general analysis of the class as a whole and more detailed analyses of pupils presenting special difficulties. Parents may be interviewed, health records consulted, notes made on truancy, fathers' occupations, numbers in families, and the contents of the school record cards. The student teacher may then concentrate on watching the pupils at work, asking pupils about their interests and aspirations and questioning pupils on the basis of a mentally pictured interview schedule. He may then listen to the pupils as they talk, read some of their work and finally he may administer a sociometric test. It would seem a pity if such an investigation were carried out *only* to substantiate what had been read in psychology and sociology books and to dispel some of the stereotypes that can emerge when pupils are classified according to the occupation of their fathers.

The main reason for collecting information about pupils we are to teach is to be able to help those pupils more effectively. Indeed, unless attention to the social factor can be seen to be of help to the child and the time spent on research by the teacher can be justified there seems little point in bothering about social psychology and sociology in teacher education. It would be quite reasonable for an efficiency expert, HMI, tutor or any member of the public to ask if time might not be better spent on other things if social investigation were not reflected in the curriculum, in the opportunities that it offers and in the increased progress that the pupils make.

However, the sensitising of teachers to social factors does not necessarily mean that a teacher will actually *do* anything. He may have all the requisite knowledge and skills needed to aid his curriculum development. He may even have a few social aims and objectives added to existing purposes but this does not necessarily mean that he will function any differently from before. This is because knowledge and skills are in themselves not enough, if the teacher does not have in addition the requisite values, attitudes and willingness to apply these.

Teaching involves intervention on the part of teachers into the learning of their pupils. In other words teacher groups and individuals seek to influence the learning of other groups and individuals. In order to do this they need to know clearly why they are intervening, what is to be achieved by the intervention, when to intervene, how to intervene and how to judge the success of the intervention. It would seem reasonable to suppose that if the teacher seeks to help his pupils make maximum progress towards their objectives (including their social objectives), purposeful intervention is more likely to achieve this if the teacher knows his pupil as a social being in addition to knowing his score on an intelligence test and his intellectual accomplishments.

SOCIAL CONSIDERATION INSIDE SCHOOL AFFECTING THE CURRICULUM

Inside the school the teachers will form an organised body of people whose appointment has been made specifically to help the pupils and sometimes they will be supported by ancillaries. There will be a hierarchy among the teachers and some proliferation of paid responsibilities in the school as a whole and sometimes within school departments. Although teachers may come together for consultation and discussion of the curriculum, for teaching purposes they will nearly always disperse into their separate classrooms. It may be questioned whether this situation is a matter of tradition rather than of adjustment to modern needs but there can be little doubt that the effect of a teacher going into such a set situation will mean that to some extent his role, and how he plays it, is prespecified. In addition, his place in a hierarchical organisation is likely to affect the influence he can exert on the school curriculum and he may have to seek change through influencing other teachers higher in the hierarchy, or risk the dangers to the pupils, the school and himself in striking out on his own path towards his own aims.

The pupils are a factor that most teachers will in any case be taking into account in their teaching, but it is well to remember that they will continue to affect the curriculum in action. They will be providing constant feedback to the teacher to which he will need to respond by changing or modifying opportunities and objectives.

A caring school community, in which teachers, pupils and ancillary staff work together and respect one another, results in a good social climate with its relaxed social relationships which aids the achievement of objectives. It often enables the teacher to concentrate on the learning of his pupils rather than on keeping order, and it makes education more attractive and rewarding. It also makes for greater freedom from social conflict and for freedom to experiment.

SOCIAL FACTORS OUTSIDE SCHOOL AFFECTING THE
CURRICULUM
(Professional and non-professional)

When the pupil first arrives at school his learning will already have been influenced by his home life and its cultural background, by the influence of relations and neighbours and by those with whom he plays. His behaviour will have been adjusted to his pre-school world. The teacher in a reception class will find that all her pupils, even at the age of four or five, are different and present unique problems. This calls for the teacher to consider to what extent common objectives for the whole class would be reasonable, whether the weighting of objectives should in all cases be the same and whether the same approach should be used for all pupils.

At one extreme an infant teacher may find herself faced with a pupil who is destructive, emotionally disturbed, unco-operative and able only to grunt a few words, while at the other extreme she may find herself with what she feels is a model pupil who can already read quite well. If the teacher wishes both these children to progress and achieve success, recognition and acceptability within her class, then objectives, approach and evaluation will certainly have to be modified for them.

In the case of the teacher in a reception class much of the pupil's learning, or lack of learning, will have resulted from social and physical conditions in which he lives and which are likely to continue to influence his learning after he has entered school. Teachers in the secondary school also have pupils whose differences are partly fostered by conditions outside school and which need to be taken into account.

Many of our schools do not draw from very mixed populations and the result can be that physical segregations within the population of the country as a whole are reproduced within many schools, and even occasionally continue to be perpetuated by the modern trend of building large estates of houses designed for a particular section of the community. So, the teacher may have pupils who by such circumstances have been isolated from other pupils by reason of their fathers' occupations, by their parents' incomes, by their parents' religious convictions or by the colour of their parents' skins. This will affect pupils' learning and make the achievement of some social aims and objectives particularly difficult for the teacher especially with regard to social attitudes, for distorted views are easily acquired about people with whom you have little or no social contact and communication. In these circumstances the teacher will be concerned, even in the case of very young children, with deviant behaviour fostered by myths expressing distrust and perhaps hatred of other members of society.

The above are factors which the teacher may or may not take into account, as he wishes, when planning a curriculum, but there are other factors which the teacher may find it difficult or even impossible to ignore. Parents in face-to-face situations or through parent-teacher associations can exert considerable pressure. The government itself can exert pressure on local authorities and through them on teachers. Local inspectors who see their role as one of direction rather than of advice can exert pressure to adopt certain answers. There are research bodies which publish papers on their findings, educational journals, salesmen of books and apparatus and those who control external examinations.

All this means that the teacher of today is faced with a greater variety and a greater intensity of influence from outside school than ever before. The outside sources of influence are better informed than previously and expect more of the teacher.

LEARNING INSIDE AND OUTSIDE SCHOOL

From the pupil's point of view there are two settings for learning—school and the outside world. Both settings will provide him with opportunities to learn. One assumes that the school will have carefully worked out aims and objectives and that the learning will be carefully organised and sequenced through interrelated opportunities with careful checks on progress and provisions for remedial opportunities where necessary. Education here is consistent and created to fulfil definite, known purposes and it functions in a purpose-built environment. In the world outside, on the other hand, learning is usually not really organised at all and the aims can only be inferred from the opportunities presented and the associated systems of reward and punishment or from what is ignored, or just accepted. In this second setting there is no means of overall control and much of what happens is by chance rather than design. As for the design of its learning environment, few would claim that it usually shows much responsible regard for the needs of children.

The point has already been made that what happens and what is learned outside school affects the school curriculum and teachers hope that their efforts in school also filter back to the outside world and affect happenings there, so that influence goes both ways. Sometimes efforts are made to join the two aspects of learning together and so form a total curriculum for the pupil. This happens when parents and teachers consult one another and work co-operatively along pre-arranged lines. Ideally, this would involve an agreed measure of unity of ideas and unity of purpose even if different ways were used to attain these purposes. It would involve agreement and overlap between what parents, society and teachers seek to achieve.

CONFLICT OF LEARNING INSIDE AND OUTSIDE SCHOOL

There is, however, little sign as yet of such agreed measures being *actively pursued* by parents, teachers and society. In fact, the picture previously presented of schools working consistently to achieve progress for all pupils to agreed and reasonable aims with related assessment and evaluation is by no means true of all institutions. It can be very tempting to have certain school aims because they may be thought to be desirable or expected. It may be felt that social pressure, for instance, demands that the aim 'to develop the character of each pupil' be included. On the other hand local judgement of the success of a school may rest in terms of success in examinations, but some heads in the present educational climate would not like to see passing examinations stated as a school aim. When this happens there is a degree of discrepancy between what teachers say they wish to foster and what their own behaviour may be seen to be fostering.

It is not suggested that teachers do this purposely. Many do not realise the need for curriculum consistency and do not check that the social and physical situation they have analysed, the aims and objectives, the approach and evaluation, all need to be linked and not seen in isolation. Others think that consistency exists but make no attempt to assess progress assuming that what they do *automatically* gives the results desired. A teacher recently assured one of the present writers that one of her aims was 'To develop the ability to work co-operatively.' It was pointed out to her that she had previously said that she *always* did class teaching and was asked how this linked up with her stated aim. The reply indicated that she often *told* the pupils to work with one another when they were outside school. She seriously believed or had faith that her exhortations would produce the desired learning and behaviour. It could be that for this particular person, who was highly respected by her pupils, her words themselves would be sufficient to influence the behaviour of her pupils, but we shall never know. As she never gave the pupils the chance to practise the social skill she sought to develop she would not know the needs of the pupils concerned, she could not check on progress and she could not identify and help those who might have been having difficulty. In fact, it is possible that constant and never-ending class teaching could be seen as a means of inhibiting rather than aiding progress towards the desired aim.

If at times there is inconsistency in the workings of the school itself and inconsistency between its teachers and even on occasion inconsistency within a single classroom, there is also a lack of consistency outside school. This is far more marked than school inconsistency. All teachers know of the parent who says that he is keen to help his child to read yet does not provide books at home nor give encouragement to read books taken from school. But parents are not the only social influence outside school and even if they are themselves consistent they may be in conflict with other social influences on their children. In particular they may be in ideological conflict with local peer groups with whom their children associate, with models presented and rewarded in television programmes, and with ideas presented in books and magazines.

In view of such a lack of consistency inside and outside school and of such conflict between school and society values, we are perhaps lucky that more pupils and teachers do not become nervous wrecks as different influences try insistently to pull or push them in different or even opposing directions.

Progress is most likely to be attained when there is consistency and agreement among teachers about the school curriculum, and agreement and co-operation with pupils and outside social influences. If it is impossible to get agreement with outside influences, at least there should be agreement among teachers themselves. In this way we may avoid the situation in which, say, one teacher functions in such a way as to encourage increasing pupil control over learning while the teacher in the next class encourages pupils to do as they are told. Also to be avoided in the search for teacher agreement is the situation in which one functions to encourage the assimilation of facts while another encourages ever higher levels of working.

Teachers, parents, society in general and certainly older pupils, will need to exchange views in an effort to get a measure of agreement about educational problems. Such agreement is likely to involve compromise. For example, on the one hand parents might support more positively than some do at present the aims and approaches of the schools. On the other hand, teachers might be more willing to take into account rather more than many do at the moment the social learning, wishes, abilities, etc. of the actual individual children they teach. If education is eventually to become open to the extent of being a partnership of all interested parties, it is most unlikely that the partners will accept dictation from any of their members, and increasingly teachers will be called upon to justify what they do in reasonable and understandable terms. In particular, the public is not likely to accept justification if it is only philosophical or in terms of teacher belief. Ultimately teachers will need to be able to show that progress has been made towards agreed aims. This sort of justification can come only from a curriculum which has been both deliberately created and tested. Moreover, if the partnership eventually materialises it will require open lines of communication.

THE NEED FOR OPEN LINES OF COMMUNICATION

In a school situation in which students, teachers and parents may have different or even opposing ideas about education, the possibility of unhelpful conflict is apparent. When schools were self-contained institutions and a law unto themselves and when head teachers exercised more individual control over the curriculum, there may have been a greater acceptance of authority on the part of pupils, teachers and parents. Parents are now invited to express their opinions and pupils are encouraged to take a greater part in their own education. Teachers are beginning to contribute more of their own knowledge, beliefs and expertise to the curriculum as the head teacher's role changes and he becomes more of a co-ordinator and facilitator. The more open the education, the more important would seem to be the call for a helpful climate in which differences may be examined and resolved. This is particularly so within the school itself, where lines of communication between the head, staff and pupils need to be open and readily usable so that there is a steady and fairly regular feedback among the parties concerned and also within those parties. The pupils and parents will no doubt tend to rely on informal lines of communication while those of the staff may be regularised, but there will be a need for provision for inter as well as intra channels of communication.

One problem demanding a good climate and open lines of communication could occur when there are on a staff teachers or groups of teachers who ask for different behaviours from their pupils. One of the writers can remember a conversation in a staff room which went like this:

1st Teacher: I seem to have lost my touch. I know the class I'm teaching is new to me and that I'm new to it, but during the last week nothing seems to have gone right. The pupils can't move about the room without making a noise and disturbing others, they can't work with one another without loud arguments, the work seems to have gone to pot and, what is more, they will keep bothering me with silly questions like, 'Can I sharpen my pencil?' or 'Can I get a book from the library?' or 'Can I go to the toilet?'.

2nd Teacher: I'm not surprised. I spent last year trying to get them to sit down quietly and get on with the work I gave them. If I gave the class work, I made sure that they always had whatever materials and books they needed given out before the class started; as for talking and movement, I was interested in what each individual child could do and not what he could copy from others or in the amount of time he could waste disturbing the lesson for everyone else.

The authors do not think it possible to discuss, praise or condemn the above different approaches to education embodied in the words of the two teachers without a deep knowledge of the objectives involved and of the existing situation in which those objectives were being sought but, whether the two teachers were trying to reach the same objectives in different ways or to reach different objectives, the result was confusion that might have been educationally unhelpful and might have caused strife among the staff if relationships and the climate had not been good.

It will be appreciated that as education becomes more open to a wider range of influence and if the role of the teacher increasingly involves the giving of advice rather than directing, so social communication will play a larger part in school life. In many schools now there is increasing contact with parents, and in the classroom the direction of verbal interaction is increasing among the pupils as they help one another. To parents who went to school many years ago pupil talking to pupil could seem like deviant behaviour and they may well wonder why teachers are often seen positively encouraging one pupil to help another when they were always expected to do their own work, with any help, if given, coming from the teacher. If the lines of communication were fully open with the teachers such parents would already know the answer, and know how they, as parents, could be of help.

THE TEACHER AS A SOCIAL FACTOR

In addition to planning the curriculum on the basis of known aims and objectives after a thorough investigation of the prevailing situation, the teacher needs to take himself into account. The teacher is a social aid for learning. He controls much of the reinforcement within the class though he can also call on the help of the pupils to reinforce the behaviour of their peers. He can use group forces to his advantage and modify the curriculum as a result of feedback. The teacher needs to know his own abilities in order to be able to adapt his approach to take into account his own as well as pupil differences. Few will disagree that the teacher should act as a model with whom the pupils can identify when they are reaching out in the direction of cognitive objectives, but teachers may care to ask themselves whether they should act or indeed whether they can avoid acting as a model when it comes to social/moral issues.

A teacher's knowledge of social psychology and sociology might help him to deal with social forces and to use social learning. He will gather social information in order to help him make a contact with and understand his pupils. He will know the value of social communication and how this can be put to use. He will know and be able to use measures of social maturity, social adjustment, social interaction and sociometry. He will know and be able to take into consideration the findings of social psychology. All this can then be used in order to help his pupils attain their objectives through approaches which take into account the assessed needs of particular groups and individuals. Such knowledge and skill, if applied, could bring a certain humanity to the curriculum.

Social influences may help the teacher or present him with problems. They may also present both help and problems to the pupil who finds that social factors influence the whole of his learning, although they are not always consistent as many of the interested parties (sometimes the teachers themselves) seem to be pulling in different directions. It is hoped that a greater measure of consistency might be achieved in the future.

Chapter 4

Some Psychological Considerations

In spite of psychology being a new and underdeveloped science which, for many reasons, often cannot be instantly applied by teachers, it nevertheless forms part of all initial courses of teacher training. The student teacher learns not only of psychological findings but additionally of how those findings are made and the relevance of psychology to the increasingly difficult task of teaching. Presumably the learning of psychology is to help the teacher to construct his curriculum and to facilitate the faster attainment of objectives by even slow-learning pupils, while at the same time helping him to avoid to some extent the teaching mistakes of the past.

Perhaps because of the newness and difficulties of the subject together with the practicalities of actual teaching, the full impact of psychological considerations has not yet been apparent in many classrooms. Eventually, however, psychological influences will have a greater effect on what pupils are taught, how they are taught, and how they are assessed.

This chapter deals with some psychological considerations and covers some points which may be helpful to the teacher and may go some way towards giving him initial guidance.

EXISTING PUPIL LEARNING

When a teacher meets his pupils for the first time they will already have acquired knowledge, skills, attitudes and values. In effect, they will have attained some objectives. Much of this learning will be helpful to the teacher and will form a base from which he can build. However, he will never find two pupils with identical learning. Indeed, there will be large learning differences existing *between* different pupils and uneven learning *within* individual pupils.

In order to help his pupils the teacher needs to diagnose accurately not only the differences that exist but also the potential of the pupil. Furthermore, the teacher needs to know something of the physical and social factors that have affected learning in the past and which may continue to do so in the future. By acquiring knowledge of his pupils the teacher is then in a better position to design curricula to lead them from where they are to where he wants them to go. He will know more clearly where he has to:

1. initiate new learning
2. further learning already started
3. speed up learning
4. correct deviation.

JUSTIFICATION FOR PSYCHOLOGY

Psychology may be thought to justify its inclusion in a teacher-education course since it generally assumed that it helps a teacher in his work. This assumption needs to be examined carefully. If psychology can help a teacher to see what may be relevant to pupil learning when he carries out his analysis of the situation, if it can help him in the selection of appropriate aims and objectives, if it can help him to create successful opportunities and if it can help him to devise assessment techniques, then it might be said that psychology justifies its inclusion.

However, another aspect of justification is the priority given to psychology over other subjects. Time is precious in a teacher-education course and one must question whether psychology is of more potential value to a teacher than other subjects. Is it more valuable for instance, than a 'method course' which offers to students set ways of teaching subjects to children of a given age range?

If it justifies its inclusion in a course, a decision has to be made about the amount of time to be devoted to psychology. One consideration must be the demands of other subjects, but in the last analysis the amount of time allocated should be justified in terms of the needs of students as potential teachers.

CHARACTERISTICS OF EDUCATIONAL PSYCHOLOGY

The fact that it is called 'educational' psychology makes it obvious that: (*a*) the range of study is restricted; (*b*) it is meant to be useful and not just an academic study. In general, psychology may be seen as an integral part of a course for teachers to be carefully woven into the whole of teacher education and assessed, for the most part, in terms of intelligent and sensitive curriculum development and teacher behaviour in the classroom.

Moreover, the psychology learned should be transferable to a particularly wide range of, if not all, learning situations. Without further teaching qualifications teachers go from city areas to rural areas, from posts in special schools and classes to ordinary schools and classes, from British schools to foreign schools, from secondary schools to primary schools and from infant schools to colleges and universities, etc. In all cases the teachers are expected to be able, with the help of their knowledge of psychology, to create efficient and justifiable curricula.

THE NEED FOR STUDY IN DEPTH

The point has been made that educational psychology is restricted to a consideration of those parts of psychology that may be of help to teachers. The word 'restricted' is not intended to give the impression that there is little to learn nor that a superficial understanding is sufficient.

Only after considerable study in width and depth can most students understand the terminology used and the possible implications of psychology for their own behaviour in creating and modifying curricula and teaching. Unless there is study in depth of the interrelated considerations of psychology, such matters as the stereotyping of pupils on the basis of their fathers' occupations and the judgement of potential solely on the basis of what is assessed by intelligence tests is a strong possibility. Moreover, the student with only a superficial understanding could believe that research has *proved*, for example, that the initial teaching alphabet is the best way to teach reading and that *all* classes should be run democratically. Lack of deep study would bring about the fear that an attempt might be made to make maximum use of psychology with a minimum of knowledge, understanding and expertise.

Before he leaves college the student teacher needs to be able to question intelligently what he reads in psychology and curriculum development books and hears from his tutors. He needs to be able to question research findings and to know the possible relevance of those findings in the unique teaching circumstances, with their unique sets of variables, in which he will function.

He then needs to be able to transfer what he knows of psychology to the classroom. This transfer is most likely to occur if the initial learning is thorough, if the possibility of transfer has been recognised, if transfer is an accepted aspect of learning and if such transfer is helped (where and when necessary) by the tutor. If there is only a little, superficial learning to transfer due to a failure to study in width and depth, there may be a good case for not learning psychology at all.

DIFFICULTIES A TEACHER MAY FACE

Having indicated the need for study in depth it is suggested that the study and practical use of psychological considerations should be spread over at least three years of a teacher-education course. This is to allow not only considerable study, but also lengthy purposeful discussion and mature consideration which comes with time and practice. This may mean that during the first teaching practice there is likely to be a considerable need for stop-gaps, practical help and suggestions from tutors which will progressively diminish with increased student learning and practice and as the student begins to know more of his own competencies and shortcomings.

This practical difficulty of lack of initial knowledge and expertise is to be expected but what is not always appreciated are the problems of learning psychology. The subject is still seeking to establish itself as a science and not all its findings and concepts are readily applicable or even generally accepted. Some findings can generate emotion which makes the exercise of rational judgement difficult and makes the same psychologist a hero to some teachers and a knave to others.

In indicating some of the difficulties in studying psychology, it would be wrong to omit the fact that it can be intellectually very demanding and that it is just not possible to miss out difficult parts from the teacher-education course. A case in point could be the study of motivation. The topic is difficult but important. The following are some reasons suggested for its inclusion:

1. The possibility that knowing what causes, cues, or develops behaviour may be helpful to the teacher.
2. The unwillingness of some pupils to stay on at school.
3. The increase in the size of pupils and decline in their willingness to submit to authority.
4. The decline in teacher status and power.
5. The fact that teachers are no longer able to rely on fear and examinations to keep order.

If some or all of the above points are valid, motivation cannot be excluded.

If a teacher is going to a different school or is teaching different individuals and groups in the same school, there is no educational recipe for how motivation or any other psychological considerations ought to be taken into account. Some ideas may come to mind as he assesses the situation. Then, *knowing the pupils,* he may be able to think out at least elementary ways of taking into account a possible need for small steps, for attainable goals, schedules of reinforcement, interests, the structuring of the situation, success with satisfaction, etc. The actual teacher plan will depend on many factors including practicalities. The teacher with a small class of twenty pupils will often be able to adjust more to individual pupil differences than one with forty. Mature pupils will offer greater opportunities for teacher experiment than those younger and less self-controlled. If a teacher has his class working together in a class group, then patterns will be different from those situations in which pupils have individual work contracts and are allowed to proceed largely unsupervised in a variety of school areas and class work bays. But even if he is attracted by one particular school of psychological thought the sheer practicalities of most learning situations mean that a teacher has to be eclectic.

Psychological considerations are for those teachers who wish to create curricular improvements which take into account the actual pupils being taught. They are for those teachers who wish to produce humane, caring curricula designed to help *all* pupils achieve success in their school life. After all, pupils should now be able to expect (when teachers have the necessary materials and facilities) an education that takes their individuality into account rather than one which gives them the same identical processing as all the others in the same class-room. Teachers might well create their curricula taking psychology into account on the grounds of the possibility of increased progress to a wide range of cognitive, affective and psycho-motor objectives and on the grounds of equal respect for all those being educated. This is to be preferred to situations in which teachers take their actual pupils into account only when forced to do so because of breakdown in social discipline or when slow-learning pupils cannot make average progress.

FACTORS WHICH MAY INHIBIT CREATIVE TEACHING

1. When the teacher was a pupil he did not have his creative potential developed.
2. His own teachers never took his differences into account.
3. His own teachers had a restricted view of education.
4. He is really only interested in his subject.

5. He is expected by those in authority to do as he is told or to follow without question an established pattern.
6. He has an easy class.
7. He believes that psychological considerations are only for slow learners.
8. He tried something different once and it did not work.
9. Creative teaching requires more teacher effort, more knowledge, more understanding and higher-level skills.
10. An examination has to be attempted by his pupils and so all the *different* pupils are given the *same* opportunities in the belief that they then have *equal* chance to pass.
11. There is difficulty in transferring his knowledge of psychology into terms of teacher behaviour. For example:
    (a) He knows that attention spans vary but does not realise that after he has been talking for five minutes John Smith always seems to switch off and therefore needs an approach which takes this into account.
    (b) He knows that readiness is a factor to be considered but fails to take levels of word recognition and comprehension into account when giving out geography books. Nor does he appreciate that after pupils have played football or after a pupil has been ill all night they may not be in a suitable mental state to tackle a difficult translation.
12. He likes to apportion blame for lack of success rather than seek to find and eliminate the cause.
13. His headmaster never comes to see what he is doing and praise him for his efforts.
14. He feels insecure.
15. Other teachers may think he is 'trying to make a name for himself'.
16. He is unable to handle a flexible situation.
17. To take psychology into account would mean a virtual revolution and even different books and apparatus would be needed.
18. He only has the pupils for three short periods a week.

SOME OF THE CURRICULAR ADJUSTMENTS THAT MAY BE NECESSARY AS A RESULT OF FEEDBACK FROM PUPILS

The changes may be necessary in relation to the whole school group, the class, sub-groups within the class or individuals.

1. Increase or decrease in the rate of attainment of objectives.
2. Change in the aims and objectives.

3. Increase or decrease in the difficulty of objectives.
4. Increase or decrease in the size of the learning steps.
5. Modification of the nature and range of activities through which it is hoped discoveries will be made.
6. Change in curricular emphases.
7. Change in what is being studied.
8. Modification of the length of time a pupil is expected to concentrate on one particular activity.
9. Modification of pupil and/or teacher roles.
10. Change in the learning areas that can be used freely by the pupil(s).
11. Change in the organisation.
12. Modification of the range and availability of materials.
13. Change in the length of the learning period.
14. Change in what is assessed and the form of assessment.

The teacher in assessing the situation, devising aims and objectives and considering assessment and evaluation does not then create opportunities which become straitjackets for himself and his pupils. He does not note pupil failure and do nothing about it because it would involve changing his plans. Nor does he stop trying to improve the curriculum and ignore the use of unplanned opportunities which arise during the course of his teaching possibly as a result of pupil feedback.

TEACHER QUESTIONS

A general knowledge of psychology and knowledge gained during the analysis of the physical and social situation as it affects individuals and groups may help to answer the following questions or even to some extent prevent such questions arising.

1. Why didn't the pupils enjoy their task this morning?
2. Whatever shall I do when my pupils no longer receive passively whatever work I give them?
3. How might I be able to encourage A—— to want to work?
4. I have pupils who have individual differences but what might this mean in terms of objectives, approach and evaluation?
5. How might *I* be motivated to use my knowledge of psychology and psychological skills when devising learning opportunities?
6. How might B—— be encouraged to continue studying after leaving: my class; school; college; university?

7. What are the psychological conditions usually necessary or desirable before C—— is ready to proceed to new, more difficult objectives?
8. D—— and E—— both have the same intelligence quotients so why shouldn't they have the same objectives, approach and competitive assessments?
9. Why are my pupils at times so dependent on me as a giver of orders and *the* centre of knowledge that they cannot proceed for more than two minutes on their own? Why do they stop working when I am not in the room?

The above questions may be asked by many teachers in vastly different teaching situations both in Britain and in countries overseas. There are no set answers but there could well be common psychological considerations of attitude, potential, attainment, readiness, motivation, personality, etc. which may be helpful in arriving at answers as the teacher creates and modifies curricula.

PSYCHOLOGY AND OPPORTUNITIES

The following are just *some* possible questions that a teacher may feel relevant as he creates opportunities. They could often also reasonably be asked *of* the teacher by tutors, heads of schools, inspectors, knowledgeable parents and others interested in custom-built education rather than continuous common processing.

1. Does the designed opportunity make use of existing, diagnosed patterns of motivation and/or are reasonable provisions made for rousing motivation?
2. Although there may be a degree of failure, is there sufficient provision for overall success and satisfaction?
3. Is there provision for the progressive shaping of behaviour?
4. What is to be the model teacher behaviour?
5. Is the pupil ready intellectually, socially, emotionally and physically for what the opportunity requires of him?
6. Is the pupil prepared to use his knowledge and skills to make full use of the opportunity?
7. Is there provision for feedback and the modification of the opportunity by the teacher and/or the pupil?
8. Does the opportunity really provide for the planned maintenance of attained objectives, and/or the stretching and developing of pupil potential in order to reach towards a range of knowledge, skills and attitudes?

9. Has the pupil's personality, span of attention and style of learning been taken into account?

10. Has provision been made for the pupil to have sufficient time to complete his work?

11. Has provision been made, where necessary, for the pupil to receive help in transferring what he has already thoroughly learned so that he can tackle the more demanding problems inherent in the new opportunity?

12. If two or more pupils have common learning opportunities, is there provision for those who attain the desired objectives to move ahead?

13. If two or more pupils have common learning opportunities, is there provision for those who do not attain the desired objectives to have further opportunities?

14. Does the opportunity depend on
    (*a*) fear of the teacher
    (*b*) established pupil working habits
    (*c*) a coming examination
    to maintain discipline rather than on good teaching?

15. Does the opportunity reflect actual diagnosed knowledge of the pupil and the social and physical settings in which he functions?

16. Is an opportunity designed for a large group intended to achieve known objectives using, perhaps, considerations of social psychology, or is it designed for the teacher's convenience with no reference at all to psychology?

17. Each pupil in the class has a different opportunity. Is this because of a skilfully designed and monitored plan? Is it based on known psychological factors and considerations? Is it the blind copying of someone else's ideas with the faith that they will work automatically to attain vague unspecified aims from all pupils, whatever the learning situation?

18. Do the opportunities take into account the psychology of only some pupils?

19. Does the opportunity reflect knowledge of the pupil or expectations based on the occupation of its parents?

20. Does the opportunity reflect reference to more than a single psychological consideration, say intelligence?

21. Do those pupils who look at their education see it as generally being in line with their wants and needs rather than an unwanted, irrelevant imposition which sees them neither as individuals nor as social beings?

22. Is the opportunity adjusted wherever appropriate so that the pupil learns with understanding?
23. Is the pupil being required to work merely on the attainment of low-level knowledge objectives with a view to subsequent regurgitation based on memory? Alternatively, will the opportunity be for the learning of facts and related concepts that can then be skilfully used by the pupil, thereby forming a base for the tackling of new, more difficult problems in the future?
24. Is the opportunity generally in line with agreed principles of learning?
25. Does the pupil work *in* a group or *with* a group that has been purposefully chosen?
26. Are there accepted and open channels of social communication?

SOME POSSIBLE INDICATIONS OF LACK OF PSYCHOLOGICAL CONSIDERATIONS

1. The group always has the same objectives for all its members.
2. All the different group members are given identical learning tasks.
3. The teacher is teaching in exactly the same way this year as last year.
4. Some pupils always seem to find the work too easy while others always seem to find it too difficult.
5. A comment in a school report which reads: 'John is not able to keep up with the work of the class.'
6. The assessment procedures are invariably the same for every pupil and each pupil is always compared with all others in his class.
7. All pupils are *assumed* to have the required knowledge, skills, attitudes, etc., that can automatically be transferred in order to deal with new problems.
8. The school is devoid of visual stimulation.
9. There is a lack of variety in the way the pupils are encouraged to learn.
10. All pupils in a secondary school class are working their way through the same pages of the same textbook.
11. All pupils in a primary school reception class (even if they can already read) are forced to work their way through reading readiness material and then through a set reading scheme.
12. Too large a proportion of the school is following the same programme series on television or radio.
13. Reports sent home impress parents with how poor their son is.

14. The pupil finds himself always compared with his elder brother or other members of his class who are more able than himself.
15. The teacher appears to work on the assumption that the more able pupils benefit from continual success while the less able benefit from continual failure.
16. Reinforcement is by chance rather than by design.
17. The teacher is obviously only really interested in his subject and/or a few of his more successful pupils.
18. There is a poor working climate.
19. The pupil is always prevented from developing his potential to create novel answers and ways of looking at problems. Instead, whatever the subject and problem, he is expected to conform in his behaviour and accept meekly what he is told.

SOME POSSIBLE INDICATIONS THAT A TEACHER IS TRYING TO TAKE PSYCHOLOGY INTO ACCOUNT

Situation Analysis   It is obvious that the teacher knows his pupils and the social and physical circumstances inside and outside school affecting their learning and development.

Aims and Objectives of the Planned Curriculum   These can be seen to be carefully linked with what has been found in the analysis of the situation and also with teacher concepts of what education is all about. There is then a psychological as well as philosophical and sociological base of realistic aims and objectives.

Planned Curriculum   Being based upon the situation and realistic and justifiable aims and objectives, the curriculum provides a chance for the *pupil* and the *teacher* to experience success.

Curriculum in Action   This will not be a rigid following of the planned curriculum. Change will occur as the teacher gathers more information about his pupils, as he checks their progress towards their objectives, as the situation changes and as more discussions about the curriculum take place. Change will also take place in teacher role and behaviour from minute to minute as a result of feedback from pupils. But, basically, the curriculum implemented will bear a close resemblance to that which was planned.

Some Possible Indications of Psychological Considerations

The following list is given as an *illustration* not as a *prescription* of how a teacher takes some psychological considerations into account.

In any case, no teacher can be expected to take all psychological considerations into account at any one time.

(*a*) *Social Climate* Pupils are working smoothly, consistently and happily.

(*b*) *Memory* Opportunities provide for the maintenance of objectives as well as for progression to new objectives, i.e. knowledge and skills are retained by use rather than left to decay with time.

(*c*) *Transfer* The teacher is asking a sixth-form pupil how he tackled problems of data collection and presentation in history, music, economics and chemistry, and inquiring whether some of the knowledge and skills he acquired could be used for an exhibition for parents dealing with the problems faced by engineers in the construction of the new local bridge.

(*d*) *Readiness* The teacher in the nursery/reception class has made sure that books and wall illustrations have very large print.

(*e*) *Attention* Long periods are broken up by a variety of different activities.

(*f*) *Motivation* Some pupils are making a variety of illustrated magazines concerned with France, others are listening to Petula Clark records in French and English, listening to a BBC broadcast over headphones, reading French murder stories or using a programmed language course. The room is ablaze with posters of France and on some of the windows are humorous pictures of French men and women painted in poster colours by the pupils. All pupils are obviously achieving success with satisfaction through varied and carefully graded opportunities.

(*g*) *Reinforcement* The teacher has obviously planned his reinforcement schedules. For instance some pupils who are doing new work and are unsure of themselves are receiving considerable regular attention while others are working in the library, receiving and needing only an occasional word at irregular intervals from their own or other teachers as they pass through. It is noticed that visitors are also used in this connection and that pupil-pupil reinforcement is encouraged.

(*h*) *Feedback* The teacher is sensitive to the behaviour of his pupils. If he sees that one of them continually gets most of his maths wrong he changes the objectives and/or approach.

(i) *Development of Potential*
- (i) The teacher is obviously using her attractive apparatus to stretch all her pupils towards known objectives, changing the apparatus or its use when the stage is reached at which a certain activity is merely passing away time.
- (ii) No pupil in the class finds the work so easy that he does not really have to think.

(j) *Stage of Development*   Some of the primary children are being given the opportunity to work at the level of formal operations.

Secondary and tertiary pupils are not being expected to function at the level of formal operations. None of these pupils is expected to function at this level when tackling new areas of learning for the first time.

(k) *Counselling*   The counselling of pupils with a view to improving their reading is obviously based on a thorough knowledge of the pupils concerned.

(l) *Discovery*   Some pupils are making their discoveries through listening to the teachers, others by painting, reading, discussing, listening, smelling the vapours from a test tube, looking at the television. One is even making his discoveries as he sits quietly in a corner thinking. The nature of the activities in which the pupils engage is to some extent controlled by their preferred or most rewarding way of learning.

(m) *Punishment*   *If* any form of punishment is used to suppress undesired behaviours it is seen as a holding operation while alternative behaviours are cued and rewarded.

Assessment and Evaluation

Educational success is judged on the basis of the actual pupils, their general social and physical circumstances and the opportunities that have been created for them.

If a teacher is going to hold out a helping, guiding hand to pupils this can be done more effectively if pupils are known. If education is to be humane, pupils need to be known. Such knowledge of pupils as individuals and as members of society involves psychology. When the teacher has clearly in his own mind what is to be attained, psychological considerations in curricular construction may help to provide more success and less frustration for teachers as well as pupils, so increasing teacher job satisfaction and pupil progress, as well as improving pupil attitudes.

The use of psychological considerations involves taking pupils as they are, not as they 'ought' to be. It is for fast as well as slow learners, to be used in order to help stretch all pupils towards higher objectives and not merely to keep them interested, for interest is a means or a beginning not an end in itself.

The use of psychology does not bring automatic success, but it does hold out the possibility of success to the teacher who can take into account those parts of psychology that may be useful in his own unique situation. Psychology does not replace the need for a hard, workmanlike and consistent teaching effort, though it may guide that effort along more fruitful channels. Finally, if teachers were to take into account only pupil motivation, they could bring about a revolution in many British schools.

Chapter 5

Decision-making

Before the approach to the achievement of objectives is designed, a great deal of thinking, discussion and decision-making will already have taken place. Early discussions may have been about what education in schools should be concerned with, and these should result in a statement of an agreed general aim or aims of education which will provide the base for later development work. This could be followed by the analysis of the learning situation in which detailed information about the actual school, the pupils and their social and physical backgrounds will be recorded. This, of course, is a normal procedure when student teachers make preparatory visits to their teaching practice schools. The important point, however, is that such information should be *used* in designing an approach, and not simply noted or recorded.

Having established an agreed aim (or aims) of education and having analysed the actual school situation in which they are teaching, teachers are then in a position to formulate realistic school aims and objectives and to establish an order of priority for these. They then have a rational base on which to build an appropriate approach.

Such a use of the first steps in the process of curriculum development should help to eliminate the all too frequent tendency for schools to state that the aim of education is, say, to produce good citizens, while actually functioning solely to promote intellectual attainments. It should also help to avoid the tendency of assessing the situation and recognising the range of differences among the pupils, only to proceed by giving these *different* pupils *identical* tasks.

In this chapter the word 'approach' is preferred to 'method and content'. The notion of an approach is much wider than that of content and/or method for whereas method is usually seen as a way of learning knowledge or of acquiring a specific skill, the word approach seems more appropriate when one is concerned with the achievement of a multiplicity of objectives covering a wide range. For example, pupils concerned with local history might be collecting information, trying to understand the implications of that information, using it to construct a model of the local village as it was five hundred years ago, making illustrative posters and writing a descriptive booklet. All these activities could form part of the approach to a range of cognitive and affective objectives relating to social studies, English, art and craft. A further illustration might be given in the case of reading. Here it is virtually impossible for a teacher to say that he is using a particular method to achieve all his reading objectives or even one of them. To do so would give a wrong impression. If a teacher says that he is using the look-and-say or the phonic or the sentence method, it will often be found that such a description fits only a very small part of what actually happens and of how he actually approaches his reading objectives. In effect, the teacher of reading would be describing a complicated approach by reference only to one component. It is possible that his approach could be so wide as to involve most if not all the curriculum.

The word 'method' also seems to be unfortunately associated with a variety of educational divisions. One hears of infant, junior and secondary method; history, geography, chemistry, reading, etc. method; methods for slow learners; methods for bright pupils, and so on. One wonders whether these divisions are at all helpful or indeed necessary. They may well account for much of the stereotyped and inhibited teaching which reflects long-established teaching practices, or which simply reflects inertia. Far more effective would be a constantly modified and creative approach to objectives which seeks continual improvement in teaching. In practice teachers find that decisions which have to be taken, whether in order to reach English, mathematics, geography or over-arching objectives, will have a greater degree of common ground than of difference.

The notion of an approach to objectives may also be more helpful with classes which contain a very wide range of abilities and where teaching is not always on a class basis. In other words, as education becomes increasingly complex and is seen as a whole which is greater than the sum of its parts, so the somewhat simplistic notions of content and method tend to be less relevant. In these circumstances specialist teachers, in consultation with their colleagues, will find themselves devising approaches which link one area of the curriculum with another.

Any approach to objectives is really a hypothesis which is to be tried and tested and then modified in the light of experience and in the light of any changes which may occur in the teaching situation. The fact that aims and objectives exist, that the teacher has created an approach to the achievement of these, that he has thus made a hypothesis, does not mean that education has thereby become rigid. In the course of teaching or at the stage when evaluation is carried out, changes can still be made. The important point about the approach to curriculum planning now under discussion is that the teacher is the controller of these changes; it is he who has the knowledge and skills to make appropriate decisions.

Since each total teaching situation, which includes the beliefs and experience of each teacher, is different, it is to be expected that different teachers are likely to come to different decisions. It is sometimes difficult to convince teachers that because their decisions are different from those of other teachers it does not necessarily mean that some are right and some are wrong. It may be that some are better than others, but only time and experience will indicate this. Each decision involves making a considered rational choice. It is not a question of applying ready-made answers which can be found in a book of 'good practice', but of creating appropriate solutions to each particular problem. Those who have changed education over the years have been the very ones who did not conform to what was considered the right answer in their day but instead worked things out for themselves.

The table which follows (page 58) presents a list of possible decisions which teachers might take. The list is by no means complete and is put forward merely in illustration and to show the complexity of the professional teacher's task. Many of the areas of decision may seem quite trivial to some teachers especially if they have set answers to the questions posed. No apology is made for including seemingly trivial or elementary questions, for at times it is beneficial to consider all possible areas of decision-making. By really examining every aspect and questioning existing decisions in the light of desired aims and objectives possibly with a view to making changes, the curriculum should become a dynamic instrument of education. Such questioning is likely to avoid the danger of rigidity which is to be found among both those who consider themselves 'progressive' and those who consider themselves 'traditional' and who will not even consider other approaches, because they firmly believe they have the right answer.

In the illustration which follows a hypothetical situation is presented. The situation is one in which the staff of a school decide to increase the range of aims they wish to pursue. Implicit in this particular statement of additional aims is a particular view of education which may not be shared by all teachers. The aims are only a selection used *in illustration*, and broadly represent the concept of pupils developing as autonomous persons and as responsible members of society. They could be appropriate for pupils whose ages range from 4 to 18, but of course the level of expected performance would increase over the years and would be plotted by teachers. The ultimate hope would be that by the time pupils left school they would have a large measure of responsible control over their own behaviour and learning, and provide most, if not all, their own motivation. Additionally, it would be hoped that pupils having acquired a positive attitude to learning would be prepared to continue their own education either formally or informally.

The table indicates in the left-hand column the areas in which decisions might have to be taken in any situation. The middle column indicates the initial teacher decisions for the original statement of aims. The right-hand column shows the possible trend of teacher decisions in the light of the additional aims. Since it is necessary in the designing of approaches to take into account the particular situation rather than the 'normal' or 'average', the suggestions listed in the right-hand column are not intended as definitive answers. Decisions should be made by those who have to take responsibility for their outcomes, namely teachers. Similarly, with the aims listed below, it should not be assumed because affective aims are included in the example that all schools should have such aims. Nevertheless it is suggested that however *different* curricula may be it is likely that there will be large *common* areas about which decisions have to be taken during their creation.

Since the example aims are stated in general terms, the decisions made at this stage (i.e. before detailed planning of learning opportunities based on objectives) can only be of a general nature. In practice it will be found that even in reaching broad, general decisions of the kind indicated, some clarification of the aims will emerge and a step will be made towards their interpretation as objectives. Further interpretation will occur when they are related to particular areas of the curriculum. In the example which follows the particular interpretation of the aims is implicit in the direction of the decisions which is suggested. Since the example aims are new to the school, being additional to an existing statement of aims, they exert considerable additional influence on the general approach to learning, and, as they are clarified, decisions can be reached about the nature of that approach. Without a change in approach there is little chance of the pupils making progress in the desired directions. The table below indicates areas in which changes might have to be made and suggests decisions which could be reached in order to promote a particular interpretation of the additional aims listed below.

Additional School Aims

1. To develop the ability to bring together for use, information, materials and resources from a variety of sources.
2. To develop the ability to integrate learning from different areas of the curriculum in order to solve problems.
3. To foster in pupils acceptance of responsibility for their own behaviour.
4. To encourage pupils to make choices based on their stated judgements and values.
5. To encourage commitment to the idea of working co-operatively with others of different abilities and interests to solve common goals.
6. To encourage commitment to the notion of life-long education.
7. To develop the individual interests of pupils.
8. To develop the individual abilities of pupils.

Table Showing the Influence of the Additional Aims on Teacher Decisions

General decision area	Initial teacher decision (original aims)	Possible trend of teacher decisions (additional aims)
Teacher role in helping pupils attain objectives	Organiser of content	Organiser of opportunities. Structurer of the learning environment. Consultant. Facilitator of learning
Teacher specialisation	Complete (secondary schools). None except for music (primary schools)	Partial (secondary and primary school)
Co-operation in teaching	Little or none	Some team teaching
General teaching approach	Direct	Mainly though not exclusively indirect
Relationships with pupils	Formal. Teacher dominated	Informal teacher/pupil partnership though in the final analysis the teacher is the controlling partner

Teacher movement	Static. Usually in front of the class	Mobile. Movement round individuals and groups
Supervision	Teacher of his class	Still mainly the teacher of his class but some co-operative supervision as teachers walk about the school and pass pupils working in corridors, halls, libraries, etc.
Lesson preparation	Individual lessons carefully planned to fit into 40-minute periods	Some individual lessons but class mainly functioning as part of a large workshop
Length of learning period	40 minutes	Half day or whole day
Media through which objectives sought	Subjects	General problems, topics, centres of interest and subjects
Availability of materials and apparatus	Tight control by the teacher of a limited range of materials and apparatus. Pupils ask for permission to get anything extra that may be needed	Most materials and apparatus readily available to pupils within the class or in resource centres. Pupils get what they want when they want it with little or no reference to the teacher
Materials, books and equipment	In sets so that all pupils in a class can have the same	Small numbers of a wide range for varying uses by individuals and groups
How pupils learn	Listening to the teacher. Reading set books. Doing set exercises	Incidental to solving individual or group problems and following individual or group interests *as well as* listening to the teacher etc.

Pupil differences	Tackled by streaming to narrow the range of ability within classes and by giving extra work and help to individuals within classes to attain the class norm. No adjustment of objectives or general approach	Tackled by reference to individuals and groups with subsequent adjustment of objectives and approach where this is felt to be desirable and possible
Progress	Lock step common approach to common objectives	Variation of approach to modified objectives
Discipline	Imposed. Working to set of rules. Conformity	Self-discipline
Pupil movement	Static, during lessons	Mobile
Teaching unit	Class group	Individuals, sub-groups within classes and class group. Grouped classes
Composition of class	Streamed	Unstreamed
Where learning takes place	Classroom	Class still forms the base for learning but pupils are not restricted to working there. Pupils free to work in resource centres, halls, corridors, odd corners, etc.
Motivation	Competition with the rest of the class. Examinations. Interests roused by the teacher	Success with satisfaction for all pupils. Use of existing interests. Competition mainly with self rather than against others. Interesting tasks within pupils' capabilities. Interests roused by the teacher. Planned reinforcement

Levels of work difficulty	Pre-conceptual, concrete operations or formal operations depending on the ability of the average pupil in the class	Pre-conceptual, concrete operations or formal operations depending on the ability of individuals or groups within the class
Modes of representation	Enactive, iconic and symbolic according to the needs of the average student	Enactive, iconic and symbolic according to the needs of individuals or groups
Learning theory	Approach based on established tradition rather than on psychological theory	Mixture of social, S-R, and cognitive according to what is being learned, and by whom it is being learned
Transfer of learning (knowledge, skills, attitudes and values)	Decisions reached on the basis of what learning the average student can transfer in order to tackle new problems	Decisions reached on the basis of what learning individuals or groups of pupils can transfer in order to tackle new problems
Assessment and records	Of intellectual attainments. Traditional examinations	Assessment of progress towards the whole range of objectives. Results of individual and group progress recorded
Criteria of success	Achievement of normative objectives	Achievement of group and individual objectives

Two further points need to be made about the decisions listed above. The first is that as well as these decisions being related to the additional aims many are also interrelated so that decisions made in one area may well affect those to be made in others. For example, there are close interrelationships among teacher role, discipline, pupil movement, teacher movement, furniture and relationships with pupils. The final point is to stress again that the table is given only as an example and that many schools may well already be operating along lines similar to those indicated in the final column.

Changes in the general approach can also come about for reasons other than a major addition to aims, as in the example given here. A teacher may wish to modify his existing aims, as, for example, in the case of a teacher of French who wishes to change emphasis from seeking to encourage abilities to translate accurately from one language to the other, to conjugate verbs and to use correct grammar, to an emphasis on the use of fluent spoken French which is not necessarily grammatically perfect, on confidence in speaking the language, on a knowledge of France and its people and on a liking for both the language and the people. Such a modification of aims could have a considerable effect on the approach. There would almost certainly be an increase in the level of noise within the class as pupils practised their spoken French. The teacher might wish to encourage even the least able to speak only in French during the language periods. The stuctured situation of learning might also include films, books, magazines, talks by visiting speakers, charts, posters which are concerned with life in France and with aspects of the geography and economy of the country.

In modifying his objectives substantially, the teacher of French has to consider how this modification will affect his decisions about his general approach. Some primary teachers, for example, are being made about such matters as discipline, grouping, the nature and availability of aids, his patterns of ordering materials, his relationships with pupils, his role, and so on. In particular, if the pupils are now to learn to speak French, such learning is unlikely to be carried on in the same manner as when pupils were translating written passages.

It is not only changes in aims which bring about changes in the general approach. Some primary teachers, for example, are being moved from a building with separate classrooms to a new open-plan building. A move of this kind can force teachers to make changes in their approach. The pupils are the same, the teachers are the same, their aims and objectives may be the same, but the building, part of the situation which needs to be analysed, is so different that it dictates changes in approach. These are likely to be concerned with groupings, relationships, teacher roles, location and use of materials and equipment, discipline, where learning takes place, record-keeping and so on. Some teachers, additionally, may wish to include new objectives which they consider to be more possible of achievement in this new situation than they were in the old.

This chapter has examined in some detail the kinds of decisions which teachers need to make at one stage in the curriculum process. No attempt has been made to suggest what solutions teachers should arrive at when they consider the various areas of decision. The examples included in the chapter show the complex interrelationships which exist among the various aspects of the curriculum and indicate the extent of the changes which follow from a change in one of the factors.

NOTES

1 For a fuller discussion of the importance of situation analysis see A. and H. Nicholls, *Developing a Curriculum* (Allen & Unwin, 1972), Ch. 2.

Chapter 6

Groups and Grouping

Unless a school is very small indeed, pupils have to be divided up in some way into manageable units. These units are still, for the most part, class units within age bands, although some schools are using vertical grouping and team teaching. The question in schools is not one of whether to group pupils but rather on what basis grouping will be carried out, how the groups will function and what degree of flexibility is envisaged. This is, of course, a very important question, but some teachers see it as the prime question, and at both the school and class unit levels decisions about grouping are frequently made in isolation. The approach to curriculum development described in this book would suggest that decisions about grouping are made in relation to the desired aims and objectives and the learning situation.

Since most schools are organised in class units the responsibility for achieving objectives is in the hands of the individual or sub-groups of specialist teachers. However, if different teachers group in different ways they may well be working towards different or even opposing objectives. In such cases, as and when pupils move from teacher to teacher they will have to make adjustments to fit in with each teacher. To some extent, adjustment is unavoidable because of teacher differences, but sometimes these differences can be so great as to cause serious problems for some pupils and so it can be helpful to have a general school policy. Such a policy will almost certainly emerge if there is a school-wide curriculum planning, which avoids the kind of situation illustrated in the following example where two teachers are working in the isolation of their own rooms pursuing their own educational aims.

Teacher 1. This teacher sees his pupils as one large group and has objectives common to everyone. Emphasis is on competition and getting good marks or coming nearer and nearer to the top of the class. He sees equal opportunity in terms of everyone having the same work to do. The objectives are cognitive. Pupils who are slow learners are given extra attention by the teacher.

Teacher 2. The second teacher sees his pupils as a group and as individuals. He has some objectives which are common to everyone and others which are deliberately chosen and adjusted for attainment by individuals. He uses class teaching on some occasions and at other times uses co-operative group or individual work. Some of the groups are of an *ad hoc* nature, being formed by the pupils themselves when they feel the need arises. Whatever the objectives, the pupils are encouraged to discuss problems with their peers as well as with the teacher. The effect of discussion and co-operation is to place greater emphasis on ways rather than on results. This teacher sees equal opportunity as meaning that different pupils need different work in order to have *equal opportunity to succeed* and, where necessary, is prepared to modify objectives in order that all pupils, and not just the more able, experience success.

It can be seen that these teachers, in having different patterns of grouping, group functions and ways of tackling difference are reflecting their different values, beliefs and attitudes. The pupils will learn different things from being in different classes, including different concepts of the role of a teacher. The conflict of ideas illustrated by the two teachers is not uncommon (though not often so pronounced), especially in schools employing rigid class systems in which teachers go it alone as best they can.

It is important to note that confusion can sometimes be caused by the terms that are used to describe some groups within school, and care needs to be taken when thinking of objectives and devising opportunities. Two of these terms are 'streamed' and 'mixed ability'. In fact *all* classes are of mixed ability and a constant lock-step advance to common objectives through common opportunities in set groups can usually only really be justified in most cases by reference to convenience or necessity rather than to educational desirability.

A teacher is expected to modify his groups according to the objectives being attempted by the pupils and according to the practicalities of the learning situation. At times during the same day infant, junior and secondary teachers will adjust grouping. They may have the whole school gathered together for a short period and then follow this with class discussion and later break up into small groups within the class. Another possibility is that pupils could have individual work-allocation cards which would call at different times for the pupils to work individually, in *ad hoc* groups and later in a class group. Though expected to use grouping in an intelligent and creative way there is no book to which the teacher can turn which will tell him how to group his own particular class in order to help achieve certain groups of objectives, and each class will present its own unique problems. This means that knowledge of group pressures, the dangers of fixed roles emerging in static groups, and the problems of isolates, etc., does not lead to ready-made prescriptions and much will have to be learned by the teacher through his experience.

When objectives are agreed throughout the school, it is likely that there will be a degree of similarity between the grouping styles of the teachers, especially where over-arching objectives are involved. This by no means indicates a stereotyped educational approach, and individual teachers will still leave the stamp of their own personalities through their control of learning. In practice, the coming together of ideas about objectives and their relative importances will give the school a character of its own, reflected in certain commonly recurring educational practices. That is to say that, while teachers will group according to the actual mixture of objectives that they are trying to attain within any one learning period, an overall pattern will emerge. Even the most *avant-garde* teacher seeking a wide range of intellectual, social, emotional, physical and attitudinal objectives, and encouraging the development of each pupil as an individual learner, will at times address himself to a class as a whole, give a group of learners identical things to do, or, as in the case of assembly, draw the whole school together and expect the pupils to respond with common behaviour. But, this will not prevent an overall picture of grouping emerging nor will it prevent each *avant-garde* school being in its own way a unique educational establishment.

SOME OF THE QUESTIONS THAT FACE A TEACHER WHEN GROUPING

1. What size of grouping is to be used?
2. How are decisions to be made as to who goes into each group?
3. Is it necessary to appoint leaders for each group? Is it desirable to appoint a leader if the class as a whole group is having class teaching to pre-specified common objectives? Is a leader necessary for a group of pupils who are working near one another and helping one another, but who are pursuing individual objectives?
4. How is a leader to be found? For instance is the teacher to appoint a leader, or the pupils? Is the choice of leader to go round the group so that everyone gets a turn? Is the teacher to let leaders emerge, envisaging a situation in which the leadership position may change according to whoever has the skills that may at any time be necessary?

5. How and by whom is the group to be organised? Does the teacher wait for the pupils to learn the necessity for organisation in the course of working?
6. How might a particular teacher introduce and cope with flexible grouping when neither he nor his pupils have the necessary skills developed from previous experience?
7. How might the teacher cope with different ages and sexes when he is grouping?
8. Is the teacher to put the rejected, neglected or true isolate in the smallest group?

These are some of the questions to which teachers and students in colleges and universities may feel they need answers. However, no ready-made answers can be given which can be applied automatically in the practical situation. In order to answer the questions raised, the teacher will have to know his own ability and the pupils concerned, the objectives to be reached and the situation in which he and the pupils are to function. He will have to be able to call upon the knowledge and skills which he can transfer from his education, psychology and social psychology courses, and at times he will have to draw on his intuition. At times, he will have to acknowledge that the practicalities of the situation will force him to modify his plans.

THE USE OF THE WORD GROUP

The fact that a pupil is regarded by the teacher as being a member of a group does not necessarily mean that he has to work in close proximity with other members, that he has the same objectives, that he is working co-operatively or that he has had the same opportunity to learn created for him as the others. A teacher may have pupils doing individual work to achieve differentiated objectives and have the pupils scattered in small working areas in many parts of the school. He would still refer to them as a group when he wishes to differentiate between those pupils for whom he has responsibility and those under the guidance of other teachers, or when he wishes to set them apart in his mind from other pupils that he has working in a classroom, say discussing a projected field trip. In this respect the actual use of the word group in the practical situation can be very wide and we may find that any two or more pupils who together can be regarded for any reason as being capable of differentiation from others can be regarded as a group, whether or not they have common purposes, a leader, common tasks, common values, social cohesion, etc., whether they come together naturally as friends helping one another, or are put together by the teacher, or whether they even work in the same room. Sometimes groups may be found working co-operatively or individually in a particular part of the school and in this way there is a physical link which can be seen. At other times groups exist only in the mind of the teacher as he mentally classifies pupils when discussing them with other teachers or when planning learning opportunities.

Perhaps the link of physical and mental grouping could be illustrated by reference to a teacher who has several pupils in his secondary school class who at the age of 17 are in some respects still very poor readers. He may have discovered, through studying their written work and discussion with the pupils concerned their very limited range of reading, that they are generally slow readers, unable to pick out essential information and unable to organise their own reading and research in order to tackle particular problems. The teacher will know that just telling these pupils the difficulties he has diagnosed is not going to help much unless at the same time he is prepared to give them opportunities to improve their skills. He may make them into a separate group working in the classroom. On the other hand he could give them, along with many others, individual work so that they can work alongside (but not with) a group in the school library. He could ask other teachers to co-operate by giving them helpful tasks in other learning periods not under his control. He could divide up those with the reading difficulty among several groups working on different problems, while at the same time making sure that their work within the groups was helpful. In his mind the teacher could classify as a group those with difficulties in reading and this will help guide the opportunities he arranges for them, the physical groups in which they function and the activities within these groups.

WORKING AREAS FOR GROUPS

Even if pupils are divided up into class units this does not mean that they always have to work in a classroom and teachers often feel that many of their objectives can be more easily achieved if they encourage pupils to move about from one work area to another where they may or may not be under the direct and constant supervision of the teacher. Such can be the case, for instance, when the teacher wishes his pupils to be able to work independently, to take responsibility for some educational decisions and to develop self-discipline.

MANAGEMENT AND CONTROL

If the teacher uses groups in a creative way he may well find that he has to handle a particularly complex and ever-changing organisation. The fluid situation which can develop from trying to individualise learning to differentiated objectives through a wide variety of opportunities is something that can appear very attractive as an intellectual exercise, but in practice is very difficult to control. The setting up of a multiplicity of different opportunities, all functioning at the same time and in different parts of the school, yet all under control with all the pupils carefully monitored for progress towards their objectives, calls for more than ordinary management skills. It would be foolish to think that all teachers have those skills and the reality has to be faced that those who have them may well be in the minority. Certainly neither of the present writers would be able to manage a class of forty in this way for other than short periods of time. Yet, at times, teachers may feel that unreasonable pressure is brought to bear on them to adopt forms of grouping for which they have had no training or experience. Frequently, too, pressure of this kind may be applied without giving the teacher adequate guidance to see him over the initial period of changeover during which he may need almost constant help.

TEACHING THE CLASS GROUP

At times the impression may be given that forms of grouping in education follow fashion or established traditions rather than design based on known purposes. Indeed, the impression given by enthusiasts could be that teaching a whole class group is to be frowned upon at all times. In practice, though, it would seem that all teachers at some time call the whole class together to tell them something or to demonstrate something so that the pupils might make progress towards objectives, through listening to the teacher or through watching the teacher model. The teacher could reasonably feel that to foster a good class climate he and the whole class of pupils could, for example, join together and sing. So, for intellectual and social reasons, as well as on grounds of economy of time, there can be some justification for class teaching. However, having said that, if a teacher should find that 90 per cent. of his time is spent in teaching the class as a group he needs to ask himself whether he is ignoring inter-and intra-pupil differences and showing a marked lack of creative initiative in the use of groups to achieve realistic objectives which stretch all pupils and are yet attainable by all pupils.

GROUP FUNCTIONS

Particular groupings do not necessarily mean that the groups also function in a particular way or that objectives are reached automatically. Grouping itself will not automatically mean that the pupils within the groups are attaining or progressing towards any objectives, for what matters is not only the composition of groups but how they function and whether they function effectively. If vertical grouping is taken as an example, we can consider the essentials of putting pupils in class groups in this way. There is only one essential prerequisite and that is that pupils of different ages go in the same class. The fact that pupils of different ages go into such a class need not mean that sub-grouping also follows the same pattern nor does it necessarily mean that the class and its sub-groups work co-operatively with the more able helping the less able and the older pupils generally helping the younger. It can and does happen that vertically-grouped classes are sub-grouped on the basis of age or ability and function in such a way that co-operation is discouraged. This could be seen as a failure to take full advantage of the possibilities for the attainment of some social aims but then not all teachers who have pupils already socially competent and possessing desired attitudes and values see social aims as being of prime importance. They might argue that if the pupils in a primary school are already generally happy and socially well-adjusted the time to concentrate on social skills and attitudes may be later in the secondary school. So, a teacher in a vertically grouped class (which incidentally may be so grouped through circumstances beyond the control of the teacher) may feel that the interests of the children are best served by concentrating on and furthering intellectual aims through sub-grouping according to intellectual ability while maintaining social skills and some attitude objectives by occasional rather than constant co-operative work.

Similarly for class teaching or class sub-groups, there is no set way that they must function. Nor, for that matter, is there a set pattern of sub-grouping to be followed in the event of teachers coming together to work in very close co-operation. Creative teaching does not involve using ready-made grouping formulae. This is not to say that the teachers should not talk to each other about their problems or read books that may be helpful. But, 'How ought *I* to group *my* pupils in order to help them achieve *their* objectives and how ought *my* group(s) to function?' are questions that the professional teacher eventually has to answer himself as best he can using his own knowledge and skills.

THE NEED FOR NEW SKILLS

If a teacher wishes to change from teaching his class as a single unit to a situation in which he uses groups to take account of and to foster individual difference, it will require considerable rethinking on his part. This will be particularly so if he also wishes his pupils to pursue a wide range of cognitive and affective objectives. He will need to acquire new teaching skills in order to put his new thoughts into operation. Where, in addition, a change has occurred from streaming to non-streaming some teachers could find themselves in a position for which their initial training has not prepared them and of which they have had no experience. There is even the possibility that the pupils, if recently transferred from another school, may already have worked in a fluid learning situation and are therefore better prepared for their roles than are the teachers. A similar situation could arise if a teacher transfers from one school in which pupils sit at their desks working away quietly on set exercises to another school in which pupils move about and talk while working on a multitude of opportunities, some of which they have created for themselves, setting up *ad hoc* groups as they are needed and occasionally having a quiet chat with the teacher when they feel that his advice might be helpful. In these circumstances the teacher cannot hope that his first efforts will be free from error even if he has a good knowledge of educational theory and colleagues and a headmaster who are willing to help him.

It would seem reasonable to suggest that, if the aims listed on page 58 were part of the whole list of aims of a particular school or class, a fluid approach to grouping might be devised. This could be an approach in which groups are formed as and when the need arises, with the class working towards objectives that, where necessary, have been differentiated in order to accommodate the assessed needs of individual pupils. Differentiated paths to those objectives could be offered with pupils sometimes working as individuals and sometimes as co-operating members of groups. *If well designed, co-ordinated and controlled*, this approach could provide a framework within which most pupils would be likely to make maximum progress. It would be extremely foolish, however, to prescribe such grouping and group functioning. The teachers on the spot are the only ones who are in the position to be able to adjust their teaching to suit the actual situation in which they teach. In any case there can be little moral justification for anyone imposing upon teachers prescriptions for which they do not accept responsibility if anything goes wrong.

The teacher is a unique human being and all his pupils are unique.

It is surely preferable, therefore, for teachers to be encouraged to use their knowledge and skills in grouping and in case of deficiencies to find new knowledge and develop new skills rather than for someone else to impose answers. A teacher will know that what he is doing is far from ideal but he has to deal with things as they are. The idea is not to impose *the* answer to grouping to achieve certain aims but for the teacher to ask himself to what extent, on what occasions and how his knowledge of grouping and of a school as a social system can be utilised in his own far from ideal situation.

PUPIL POWER

A teacher can find himself in a situation in which the pupils he is teaching have been grouped together by situational circumstances rather than by design of the teacher or of the pupils. The pupils' conception of the role of the teacher and of the aims they should both have may well be at variance with the teacher's own. Such conditions are not conducive to a good climate in which the teacher can work out aims and approaches. In these circumstances the teacher will find his freedom limited by pupil power and pupil interests, and whether he wishes it or not his pupils could well be developing the power and ability to take increasing control of their own education by forcing the teacher to modify his teaching and its purposes.

In restrictive circumstances which inhibit adaptation to the changing needs and with pressures within schools, teachers could find themselves in increasing difficulty especially with the demand for the transfer of more and more power to the pupils, who are becoming less and less willing to accept a working day at school which is spent sitting quietly in class behind a desk absorbing knowledge. It is a long time since teachers thought they were, and ought to be, the sole decision takers, standard setters, distributors of tasks, and the sole determiners of (at least overt) objectives or even the sole distributors of rewards. That the teacher is often no longer the autocratic king of the castle, even in his own classroom, is a reflection of the development of certain ideas on education and social pressures. Some of the changes brought about concerning groups, work within groups and education in general are the result of thought and experiment by educationists which have become accepted as reasonable, while other changes have been due to social pressure, not the least of which has been pupil pressure. Especially with older, self-assured and larger pupils there is an increasing revolt against groupings and objectives which fail to recognise individuality and fail to recognise that they may wish to have a say as well as a part in their own education.

Teachers are increasingly coming to recognise pupil power and to realise, even without the findings of social psychology, that if it comes to a head-on clash of influence between the teacher and the groups for which he is responsible his chances of controlling learning are very much diminished. To remain the guiding influence, the teacher is having to be aware of and sensitive to groups and individuals within those groups. He needs to know their aspirations, interests and abilities and to be able to adjust his approach to his own objectives in such a way as to be able to utilise this knowledge.

The large class group has particular difficulties in this direction, especially when the objectives are, and are seen by the learners to be solely determined by the teacher who then devises his opportunities (or aims his lesson as we have sometimes heard it put) for the middle of the class. This automatically means that those who are faster are held back while slow learners may never reach the objectives at all so that when they move on to their next class they do not have well learned skills and knowledge to transfer to the new and more demanding situation.

It is hardly surprising that learners who fail to see education as reaching towards objectives which they as well as the teacher value and also as failing to provide them with success, should be inclined to opt out. If, as has been pointed out, the group or groups do opt out, or in some cases actually revolt against their education, it is usually the teacher and not so much the group(s) who will be forced to adjust. The teacher, using his experience, will have to adjust his behaviour in order to exercise control over the learning of his pupils.

Where learners are now expected to exercise a greater control over their own learning and to contribute more of their own ideas and also to help one another to learn, this of practical necessity means that there is a shifting of some power from teacher to the taught. Where there is an attempt to socialise and individualise learning this also affects the balance of power and a teacher will find that if he attempts to have a particularly flexible approach to grouping, power and leadership within the class or school will be affected, especially if that teacher envisages the learners working in a multitude of places in which they will have to exercise self-discipline. The effect is likely to be not only in the balance of power and leadership but also in how they are exercised.

SOCIALLY IMPOSED AND SELF-DISCIPLINE

Another problem to be faced by the teacher is that of discipline. Although spreading pupils over a wide learning area often helps discipline, this is by no means always true. Twenty pupils working in the library while twenty more work in the classroom gives the pupils a lot more space in which to work. In a period in which the opportunities demand that pupils walk about and talk quietly, enlargement of the work area can be an advantage, providing an opportunity for some pupils concerned to move towards the aim of self-discipline while working at the same time towards cognitive aims. It would be very nice if the teacher wishing to develop self-discipline could just say to himself, 'Working unsupervised in different parts of the school *will* help the attainment of this aim, *therefore* I will let my class move about the school and use a variety of learning areas.' No doubt working unsupervised *might* help self-discipline, and until a pupil can work in such a way he can hardly be regarded as self-disciplined, but the teacher does not just send his pupils out of his sight and expect that self-discipline will automatically result. He checks that certain preconditions are satisfied and even then he still does not expect automatic progress. Among these preconditions could be the following:

Readiness

The pupils are intellectually, socially and emotionally ready to work on their opportunities in the learning areas to be used, i.e. that they have already attained necessary and less demanding objectives so that they have the necessary knowledge, skills and attitudes to transfer. From the readiness point of view there is also the question of the immediate state of preparedness to settle down to work. For instance, a period following a games lesson may not be the time to send pupils to work unsupervised.

Motivation

The pupils are likely to find the opportunities they are offered rewarding and satisfying.

Control

The teacher can control the opportunities and at the same time check on progress.

Sensitivity to others

The freedoms of the class concerned do not interfere with the freedoms and learning of other classes and teachers.

Of course if one of the aims is to develop the ability of pupils to work co-operatively it would be wrong to think that every student in school, college and university wishes to acquire this skill, especially when it may mean working with others who are not his close friends. In this instance, pupils may in many ways be ready but also unwilling even after it has been pointed out to them that in everyday life and at work co-operation is likely to be needed. Some prefer to go their own way and stand on their own feet, plough their own furrow, competing with, rather than co-operating with others.

Even the school timetable can be seen on occasion to inhibit certain grouping and group functioning. If the day is split up into very short periods and pupils move from class to class, individual and small group work, using a variety of opportunities to differentiated objectives, is made virtually impossible. There is just not sufficient time for pupils to change classes, get out and do their different work and discuss it with the teacher before tidying up and moving on to the next lesson in another classroom.

If a variety of art materials, books and apparatus is to be used this further discourages sub-grouping and individual work within a class if the periods are short. This is especially so if those aids were originally bought with the expectancy of class teaching. Here the teacher would not have the variety of resources to call upon to aid learning. Forty identical class textbooks are more suitable for a lock step advance than for pupils with differentiated objectives and opportunities.

SOME EFFECTS OF GROUPING

Factors such as those mentioned above can inhibit grouping in order to attain certain objectives. On the other hand, some grouping could have harmful side-effects with opportunities devised for one set of aims possibly even producing regression in other areas. It may be felt, for instance, that selective ability grouping does more overall harm than good and is not to be accepted in schools even though the community as a whole outside school is in effect selectively grouped socially in different housing areas. This may be why comprehensive schools and destreaming seem now to be in favour. These usually produce a much wider range of pupil difference within schools and classes even when the selective nature of the population from which the school draws its pupils is not itself comprehensive and therefore cannot provide a truly balanced comprehensive intake. The greater skill demanded of the teacher in coping with a wider range of pupil difference is thought to be amply rewarded by the increased possibility of attaining certain social aims without putting the attainment of cognitive aims at risk. Time is needed to test fully the hypotheses implicit in comprehensive schooling at secondary as well as at the primary stage, and in nonstreaming to indicate the circumstances in which hypotheses are true and to compare the overall effect of this particular grouping with previous selective groupings.

As pupils get older and have the benefits of greater learning and maturity, so it can be expected that there will be considerable improvement in their cognitive and social behaviour. In the case of cognitive advance it will be expected that pupils will not only have had a variation in what they have studied but also in the intellectual level of their study. This will mean that whereas at the primary stage the problems to be tackled by the pupils may have to be fairly simple, at the age of 16 to 18 the majority of pupils should be capable of doing rather more in many subjects than regurgitate a list of facts from a book or depend upon their memory to repeat the teacher's set answer to the teacher's set 'problem'. Pupils will be expected to show more than memorised knowledge and comprehension in the tackling of *real* problems and in providing rational justification for their solutions. It would seem a pity if pupils who are mentally capable of working at the level of formal operations are not encouraged to work at that level. Yet maintaining progress in the level of intellectual functioning is difficult for the teacher. If he works through class teaching there is some difficulty in devising opportunities equally suitable for all the pupils. On the other hand, if he has a class of thirty and wishes to individualise his teaching he is faced with the problem of devising countless opportunities unless the pupils themselves are capable of some or most of their own. One answer for many teachers seems to be in having three or four sub-groups which are more easily handled. They know that this may not be the ideal way to secure maximum cognitive progress in depth as well as width, but they recognise that grouping is a matter of practicalities as well as theories and ideals. This is why ready-made prescription is not so helpful as individual creation.

Perhaps here there is a need for a cautionary word about the further possible effects of grouping. If the social aims outlined on page 58 were felt to be desirable for infant, junior and secondary pupils and they were pursued through a successful use of fluid grouping and individual work to differentiated objectives, by the age of 18, aided by the progressively smaller classes a pupil tends to meet as he grows older, the total effect would be marked. The pupils (or at least most of them) should be capable of a high level of self-discipline, be largely in charge of their own education in school and perhaps be helping to

set their own objectives and helping create and use their own opportunities. They should also be capable of switching from individual to
ad hoc group work according to their and other pupils' needs. In
addition the range of pupil differences would have increased considerably. It does not need the writers to point out that this is not
necessarily what happens in practice. Eighteen-year-old pupils and
students in college and university could, as a result of lack of practice
and opportunity to make progress, be less capable in many of the
above respects than 9-year-old pupils in a primary school.

There are alternatives to grouping according to the objectives that
are being attempted. The teacher can group according to a pattern
established within a school, or on the basis of what he feels are modern
trends or according to what he feels he knows and is skilled in handling. It is very easy to criticise these reasons, condemning such teachers
as rigid, or easily blown by any passing wind, or intellectually lacking,
or as being reactionary, morally weak or inhibited. These attacks seek
to change through the force of condemnation rather than by putting
forward reasonable alternatives. It is surely to be preferred that the
idea of planned curriculum development and the related idea of
groupings based on objectives is accepted as logical, reasonable,
practically possible and desirable. Moreover there is a tremendous
pressure on teachers to conform rather than to create, to accept
blindly what is done rather than to participate intelligently in what is
reasonable. It is sometimes not appreciated that pressure to conform
can exist justs as much in those schools that are labelled progressive
as in those labelled traditional. As for those teachers who prefer to
stay secure with the familiar, one may wish they would be a little more
adventurous both in seeking to know clearly their objectives and in
manipulating groupings in order to aid their attainment, but one can
recognise that their lack of adventure may be due to lack of knowledge, skills and experience or due to tales they have heard of how
some teachers have dived into flexible grouping which they could
neither understand nor handle.

It may sometimes be felt that grouping in order to reach objectives
is something new. This is, of course, far from the truth. Purposeful
grouping has been a feature of social life and education since the birth
of man. What appears to be happening now is that grouping is becoming, as life itself, rather more sophisticated. Some of its complication
is also the result of a desire in schools, colleges and universities to
attain a wider range of objectives, of a wish to make education fit
the learner and of a realisation that intelligent grouping is not only an

administrative convenience but a feature of the life of the institution that can be manipulated and used as an aid to learning. The constant desire to make education more effective makes the knowing of the objectives to be sought through the help of groups all that much more important in order to aid intelligent group planning.

It is worth remembering that it is not really whether a teacher or school will or will not group but rather what will be the nature, functioning and purposes of grouping. A wise teacher will know of the possibilities that may, under helpful conditions, be offered by, say, horizontal and vertical grouping, and streaming and non-streaming within schools, and friendship, ability, complementary skill, static, flexible, *ad hoc*, etc. groupings within classes and by team teaching. At the same time he will bear in mind some of the problems that these groupings may present and one problem that all groups present, namely that they are *all* of mixed abilities, attitudes, values and personalities.

The way a teacher forms groups and the ways in which those groups function reflect his knowledge, skills and hierarchy of values. By examining his groups he will be able to see the extent to which his grouping hypotheses are working in practice. In other words he will be able to see whether the objectives *implicit* in the formation and functioning of the groups are consistent with the objectives *desired*.

Chapter 7

Aids to Learning

The days when a teacher had only his voice, a blackboard and chalk, and large sets of books to aid him in his work have long since passed. In current times he is faced with what can seem a bewildering range of aids of many kinds, with new ones constantly appearing on the market. This superabundance of aids offers teachers considerable opportunities to make their work more effective, to release them from some tasks and to provide variety and flexibility, but at the same time it can also cause some teachers to use aids just for the sake of using them or it can bewilder some teachers to such an extent that they use very few.

The purpose of this chapter is to suggest criteria which might be helpful to teachers in their choice of aids, and to discuss types of aids and some of the factors which might inhibit their use. The word aid is used to denote anything which can help the achievement of learning objectives and which can transmit or help to transmit experiences through any of the senses.

CRITERIA FOR THE SELECTION OF AIDS

Purpose

The teacher should have a definite objective or objectives in mind when he considers the use of an aid. Aids should not be used *solely* because they are attractive or *solely* because pupils might enjoy using them.

Appropriateness

(*a*) *Time* The aid should be introduced at the time when it is likely to be most effective. Such judgement is part of a teacher's professional expertise and requires detailed knowledge of pupils' previous learning and their readiness to acquire new learning.

(*b*) *Place* Aids should be available in places conducive to their effective use, in other words, they should be kept in convenient and accessible places.

(*c*) *Difficulty in handling* The question of difficulty concerns both pupils and teachers. In the case of pupils one would expect that at certain stages some would be unable to cope with delicate, small or complicated pieces of apparatus. Similarly, if a teacher cannot cope with a particular aid through lack of experience or knowledge it cannot be considered appropriate for that teacher at that time. Even a film projector is of little use if the teacher cannot thread the film and work the controls.

(*d*) *Number* In some circumstances it is possible to get a surfeit of aids with which neither the teacher nor the pupils can cope. In this case organisation breaks down. In the infant school this suggests the consideration of the possibility of restricting the number of games, work cards, paint, glue, scissors, books, maths apparatus, building blocks and toys available at any given time. At the secondary school this problem is not likely to loom so large though a lesson period of forty minutes could impose its own restrictions on what could be made available, used and returned in the time.

(*e*) *Level of pupil functioning and previous knowledge demanded* This refers to the previous learning of the pupil or pupils that can be transferred in order to make full use of the aid. This can apply at all ages and at all stages of education and to such common aids as books which can only be effective if pupils can read them.

(*f*) *Size* Here, for example, the infant teacher may ask himself whether very small toy cars are suitable for the nursery class. Other teachers may argue the case for a 26-inch television set which is so large that many classes can view it at the same time while others put forward a case for a portable set which can be moved from room to room without difficulty and stored under lock and key in a classroom cupboard.

(*g*) *Lookafterability* This refers to the need for aids to be cared for and maintained. With the most careful use on the part of the pupil and teacher, aids do wear and breakdown. In some cases where the cost is low a replacement can be bought. Others have to be repaired and this can be educationally costly if the language laboratory, the programmed learning machinery, the television or the tape recorder are out of action for several weeks when they had been carefully built into the learning opportunities. Not all schools have a teacher or technician who can handle repairs and maintenance, though these are becoming increasingly necessary as some aids become more sophisticated. Different problems of care, but equally relevant when they are used by a school, concern such aids as the school donkey, goat, bees, hamsters and vegetable garden. Who is to look after them during the school holidays?

Availability

It may be seen as stating the obvious when one of the criteria for selection is said to be availability and yet it is easy to assume that certain aids exist when they do not, or that they can be used at any time when in fact their use is restricted. The problem is largely one for the teacher who has been newly appointed to a school and who has not yet had the list of school aids given to him and who has not yet been able to find out what aids can be obtained locally. Such a teacher could have quite a surprise when he finds, for example, that his new school does not have a projector, a photocopier or a supply of sugar paper. That same teacher could have come from a school at which the pupils could be relied upon to bring masses of material from home. This is not so in all schools. A request by the new art teacher for the pupils to bring junk from home to make models and pictures could in some cases result in a few bent nails. On the other hand, tucked away in the far corners of many teachers' cupboards are aids which never see the light of day simply because they have been forgotten. There is then a need for a rigorous checking on what aids are readily available with the possibility that such a search may unearth treasures of the past which could yet return to fashion like those black wooden slates the pupils used in the good (or bad) old days and which could prove a boon to many very modern infant teachers.

Cost effectiveness

The question to be answered is, 'Is the return in terms of learning commensurate with the cost?' To bring education down to the level of pounds and pence is, for the idealist, almost a criminal act and yet this practicality has to be borne in mind. The irksome task of paring down a requisition or of preparing a case for why one teacher or department should receive special financial consideration is part of life in schools and it is to be expected that the cost of attaining some objectives will be greater than others and that head teachers may tend in any case to allocate more money to those teachers who will make the best use of it. A teacher of a foreign language could explain to his head teacher that objectives are changing and that in order to attain these objectives he needs a language laboratory. A teacher just introducing a foreign language to a school could also say, quite reasonably, that initially, at least, he needs a rather large allocation of funds. Some subjects may demand more money for aids than others. A case in point could be science which needs many aids especially if the objectives stress understanding and independent study. It is also interesting to listen to the reasonable case that infant teachers can put forward as to why they need more money for aids than secondary teachers, but this is a battle that has to be fought outside rather than inside the school. However good a case a teacher can put forward for aids which may drastically change behaviour in the desired directions, few head teachers are going to be impressed if in the past there has been evidence that objectives have not been attained and aids have not been looked after.

To look on effectiveness in terms of initial cost only is to be misleadingly narrow in concept. The initial cost is but part of the picture and money is not the only consideration as far as cost is concerned, for there are other very relevant factors. Sets of Cuisenaire rods or a piece of machinery initially can be very expensive but if they help achieve objectives more quickly and last a long time the expense can be justified. On the other hand, if teachers buy lots of expensive machines for use with programmed learning units and then find that the machines constantly go wrong and that there is a shortage of software, or if through miniaturisation and standardisation some closed circuit television apparatus and video-tape become obsolete, or if the teacher who pressed so hard to buy a kiln and lots of expensive materials for pottery suddenly leaves, then a head teacher and those teachers who had to go without in order that the expensive equipment could be bought, have cause to be rather upset, as have those who feel that aids were bought for show or because of fashion rather than because they would help pupils to reach objectives more quickly.

It will be seen that to give all teachers or departments the same amount of money to spend on aids is unjust. To consider only the initial cost fails to take into account durability, effectiveness and cost in terms of teacher time. From choice or through lack of money many teachers spend hours of their own time making work cards, or charts or painstakingly writing and rewriting a programme for a teaching machine. This is a side of teaching that is often not appreciated by the general public and for which there will always be a need if teachers are seeking to adjust education to those who are actually being educated. Educational suppliers need have no fear that teachers of the future will make or gather all their own aids for this is not a practical possibility, but the teacher would do well to consider whether what he is doing is worthwhile from the point of view of the amount of time spent and the educational results obtained. There is a limit to both time and money and the art is in spending both wisely in the interests of the pupils. To spend months on making an English programmed text needs to be weighed against all the other things that could have been done in the same amount of time, as also the cost of a language laboratory needs to be considered against the number of books, slides, pictures, records, etc., that could have been bought for the same money.

GRADING OF AIDS

If aids are to be effective in promoting learning, grading will have to be considered and, as pupils are all different, this will mean that many are not ready for some aids while other aids have ceased to be useful. As far as books are concerned, in the distant past some primary schools would order for the whole school, and for every pupil within that school, a reading scheme that would be tied by age to a definite class. This being so, book one would be read in the first year, book two in the second year and so on. Similarly in secondary schools there were first year French books and second year French books. It was as though the pupils had to fit the books rather than the other way round. Now it is not only known but accepted that even at the age of 7 many pupils can have great difficulty with reading while, at the other end of the scale, some 7-year-olds are reading simplified encyclopedias. Quite apart from the question of whether it is advisable for a teacher to pin all his hopes on a single reading scheme, it is obvious that the quicker learner of reading could become inhibited and take far longer than is necessary for him to reach objectives. The slower learner, on the other hand, is in danger of developing a dislike for reading if only because he is not able to have equal opportunity with many of his peers of experiencing success. To help a pupil we must take him as he is, not as we feel he ought to be, and this will demand grading so that the pupil advances from a base of what is known to what is unknown in suitably sized steps using carefully selected and graded aids.

There is difficulty when a teacher is given a long syllabus with orders or expectations that all pupils have to 'cover' the whole of it. In such circumstances it is not unknown for the content to be broken up into sections and taught in lock-step fashion regardless of the progress of individual pupils. Under these conditions, where learning is hierarchical or sequential, those who cannot cope with the level of the work will not be helped by the so-called aids used. But if aids cease to be aids or even become deterrents when the level of function-

ing demanded is too high for some pupils, at the other end of the
scale aids may cease to further the progress of other pupils and act
only as a means of keeping them happy and occupied while maintaining learning rather than stretching them in the direction of further
objectives.

CHOICE OF AIDS

In many ways choice is related to grading and to the factors already
mentioned concerning criteria for selection of aids. The additional
points to be mentioned here are related to the range from which a
choice can be made and to those who should make the choice. Consider the teacher who wishes an 8-year-old to learn what is meant by
the term fraction, to learn that often one fraction can be translated
into another fraction (e.g. a half can be translated into tenths or two-
thirds into twelfths), and to be able to perform at the understanding
level simple addition and subtraction and at the mechanical level
multiplication and division of fractions. A particularly fast learning
and ready 8-year-old has been known to learn this much about fractions in twenty minutes with constant teacher attention and with aids
consisting merely of a pencil, a piece of paper and the teacher's voice.
With a slower learning pupil the teacher would have to choose from
the range of aids available those most likely to achieve success, and
perhaps also to improvise other aids. The learning period, instead of
being measured in minutes, could be, in this case, measured in years,
with the teacher patiently trying to encourage readiness and then
learning, using his professional skill, judgement and intuition in
deciding which aids to use and when to use them and constantly
changing his strategy and his aids when the pupil's attempts at learning are frustrated.

The choice of a particular aid or combination of aids is a matter
for the decision of the teacher on the spot, or sometimes of the pupil.
Each develops his expertise with thought and experience, and each
develops the ability to anticipate what will be needed and the teacher
is then able to a large extent to build in the planned use of aids when
the curriculum is developed. Where pupils themselves have an element
of control over their own learning this means that the teacher will have
to anticipate in his purchasing of aids their requirements as well as
his own. The detailed pattern of purchase or making of aids will vary
from teacher to teacher and school to school, but a *general* pattern
does emerge in each case. It is surprising how much it is possible to
know about education in a school from the orders sent in to suppliers.
It is also possible from such orders to spot changes that occur within

a school since the changes in aims and approach are necessarily reflected in changes in what is needed. A change from, say, ordering class textbooks in sets of thirty to asking for small numbers of a wide range of books or a request for the school desks to be replaced by tables of various sizes and storage lockers, are indications of major changes in educational thinking and practice.

TYPES OF AIDS

In addition to such matters as planned reinforcements, realistic objectives, school organisation, school climate, and so on, which help learning, there are many more concrete aids which the teacher can use. In fact, it would appear that the number of aids is limitless, for everything can teach us something. As far as the teacher is concerned, the art is in knowing first of all what it is hoped will be achieved and then marshalling and organising aids in order to help give the pupils improved opportunities to learn.

It is surprising to see how few aids some teachers feel their pupils need but in general the trend is for more and more aids to be used, for them to be more varied and sophisticated and for there to be a wider view of what constitutes an aid. When a parent exclaims that he keeps *telling* his child something but that he never seems to learn the teacher may smile to himself for he at least knows that telling is only one way to encourage learning. The human voice, to which a pupil can listen, is without doubt of very great help to learning but it has its limitations and is in any case making use of only one of the capabilities of the aid being used, namely the teacher himself.

The armoury of aids upon which a teacher can draw is often very extensive and this is as it should be. We know that at home the parent possibly has such things as a television (often present in even the poorest homes), books and games from which they and their children learn. In the home situation, however, learning tends to be incidental rather than the result of careful planning. At school this is not so. The learning is carefully planned and everything is angled to achieve the school's purposes, including the aids, which are not there merely to be decorative or to pass away the time. The self-loading projectors, programmed learning machines, the television and language laboratories, are examples of expensive and sophisticated aids, but the cheaper and long established aids like pictures, wall-charts, crayons, paint, paper, books and blackboards still have a major part to play. In addition, there are also available such things as maths and science apparatus, materials from Schools Council projects and educational packages from publishers. The choice of aids is ever increasing. There is also a tendency to appoint *aides*—staff are being appointed to schools to give direct assistance to teachers. There appears to be some resistance to these appointments in some quarters as they are seen on occasions as diluting the profession or replacing teachers, but it is doubtful whether there is any real cause for knowledgeable, professional teachers to feel any alarm. The greatest concern should be that these aides are used to the full. It is all too easy for a laboratory assistant to waste his time getting out and setting up apparatus when the pupils themselves need this experience, or for him to stand by for an hour while a teacher delivers a class lesson. Even in primary schools an extra person can seem to be an intrusion in a room unless her function is built into the teaching. In effect, an extra pair of hands means that a change in the total approach is necessary or, at the least, desirable.

TESTS

Tests are usually a means of assessing the extent to which learning has taken place. The results are then loosely translated into marks and recorded in such a way as to say how well the student has performed on the test. But tests can be used rather more constructively than this. If we wish to see how much actual progress has been made towards objectives then a starting point needs to be established. If objectives are to be realistic then readiness needs to be tested. This testing needs to be done *before* learning begins and it may be found in some cases that the objectives which the teacher has in mind may not be realistic for some pupils as they do not have the requisite learning to transfer to the new problems. Others in the class may already have attained the objectives even before the period of learning begins. When this information is available it can be used to modify the teaching on the basis of known strengths and weaknesses. Further testing at the end of the learning period could then show by reference back to the initial testing the actual progress that had been made, the areas in which progress had been made and the areas in which regression had taken place. This information, as with the initial testing, could then be used to improve teaching, i.e. it is a teaching aid.

THE SCHOOL BUILDING

In an emergency all sorts of buildings have been pressed into service as schools and classrooms. This does not mean that any old buildings or prefabricated units are sufficient and that all a teacher and his pupils need is the space in which to work. The need is for a purpose-built building, i.e. a building so designed as to help fulfil the purposes (the objectives) of education. By looking at old schools some idea of the changing concepts of education may be gleaned and one of the most striking features is the appearance of present-day buildings and the extent and quality of the school grounds. It is evident, even to the layman, that ideas and educational values have changed.

Pupils and teachers do need space but the new buildings show that this space is now being designed and used in different ways. The facilities for learning have changed as more subjects and wider topics are tackled and as the three Rs, though still important, are seen as part of a very much extended area of concern. In other words the designers of schools see them as aids to learning. Open-plan primary schools are presumably the result of educational ideas which they seek to promote as well as of financial economy, as are large secondary schools. Bearing in mind the change in educational ideas, old buildings present problems even when those buildings are structurally sound. A good coat of paint is not really sufficient for in many cases the whole concept of the building fails to meet the educational ideas which are at present dominant.

If the designers see school buildings as aids to learning in their own right, it is not always apparent that teachers do so. Given that teachers and designers are never likely to see completely eye to eye on what is needed and that teachers and pupils will never be completely satisfied with any building no matter how old or new it is, surely it is up to us to make the best use of whatever aids we have. If we teach in certain schools this may mean making the best use of what we consider to be a poor building job, a poor building aid. There are very few schools which, by design or chance, do not provide corners in which work can be displayed and quieter areas in which pupils can work relatively undisturbed. All schools have walls and ceilings as well as floors that can often be used to good purpose. It can be disappointing sometimes to see in some schools how little of the available space is used and how dull and stereotyped, rather than creative and alive, is the attitude to the building.

INHIBITING FACTORS IN THE USE OF AIDS

Not all teachers are enthusiastic about using a wide variety of aids and it cannot be assumed that these teachers are poor teachers. One may feel that if they were a little more venturesome and would experiment even to a limited extent their pupils would be helped, but they may honestly believe that what they would call straightforward teaching with no 'frills' is best. Certainly, few would argue that a good straightforward teacher is more likely to be of greater help to his pupils than another teacher who has a wonderful curriculum worked out directed towards a multitude of objectives and using a battery of aids, but who cannot control the situation he has created. But, many are inhibited in the use of aids for other reasons. Some are not aware of the aids that exist, some may feel that the use of aids in their schools is not really encouraged and that even to cover the walls of their rooms and of the corridors with attractive and informative posters would be regarded as showing off. There are others who lack confidence or who feel that the short school periods and the constant movement from one classroom to another make the use of aids rather difficult. There is also the question of accessibility. Neither pupils nor staff are going to make a maximum use of aids if they are not readily accessible. Indeed, a projector locked away in a cupboard and never used ceases to be an aid. Finally, there is the factor of lack of expertise on the part of some teachers, not only of the actual mechanical handling of some of the more complicated items of equipment, but also in selecting aids which can promote the desired learning.

THE SITING OF AIDS

Aids used by the teacher and pupil are sited in many different places and to some extent the amount of use to which aids are put depends on this siting and how difficult they are to get at. With this in mind it is possible to plan both where the aids will be kept and helpful procedures for getting at them. Things that are likely to be needed frequently are often kept by the pupil himself in his desk, box, cubbyhole or satchel, while stored in the classroom in cupboards, on shelves, in drawers and on tables are those things of aid to the class as a whole or to the teacher. Many aids, however, are not kept only for use in one particular classroom but are available to the school as a whole, and in this case teachers and pupils need to be able to borrow from different classrooms or to be able to go to a central store from which the aids can be used. For such purposes, most schools now have a library and at least one other resource centre.

There are resource centres outside school which can be called upon or visited. Local authorities often set up large centres upon which all their schools can draw. Local authorities also have large libraries and museums which pupils can visit; many schools extend their area of operation outside the building and grounds of the institution to visit these centres of aid. Some schools go even further, visiting farms, castles, and factories, doing field-study trips or even visiting foreign countries. The idea is that if the aids cannot be brought to the pupils then the pupils are taken to the aids. Through the use of the increased number and range of aids, pupils now have open to them many extra ways of achieving objectives, offering many new ways of learning through a variety of attractive activities. Some aids can release the teacher from certain tasks and allow him to give extra attention to those pupils who are in need of help. When a sufficient range of suitably graded aids becomes available, thereby making a lock-step advance unnecessary, teachers should have a real opportunity to individualise learning. When this happens increasing numbers of pupils will reach more and higher objectives.

Chapter 8

Organisation for Learning

A teacher who has analysed carefully his situation, determined aims and objectives, and created related learning opportunities, then has to work out how the class as a whole is going to function. He already has in his mind a model for the development of curricula and he now has to create a model for his own particular curriculum in action. His task here is to co-ordinate the activities of people and the use of time, space and materials in order to achieve maximum efficiency, continuous progress and the linking of various educational parts to form a whole. At the same time, his detailed comprehensive plan needs to make provision for further curriculum development.

A considerable amount of pre-planning is necessary before the curriculum is put into action. This is particulary so in the kind of complex and fluid situation which now exists in many schools. It is not suggested that every minute detail has to be planned and organised in such a way as to allow no flexibility for either teacher or pupils. Flexibility is highly desirable, as is the chance to use events and circumstances as they arise, but the notion, if ever it existed, that a teacher can carry out all his organisation as he walks into the classroom is now dead.

The head teacher's role in organisation is a particularly important one since his responsibilities affect the whole school. Decisions made by him may affect aspects of the organisation of every class: such decisions would include the way the timetable is organised, the manner in which pupils are grouped and the way in which resources are allocated. Especially in larger schools, the head teacher frequently delegates some of his organisational responsibilities to other members of staff in the interests of increased efficiency.

In the classroom a teacher may also delegate responsibility for aspects of organisation to pupils. On occasions this might also be in the interests of greater efficiency in a highly complex situation, but it might also be in the pursuit of certain objectives such as those concerning pupils' responsibility for their own learning, co-operation with others and consideration for others.

Reference has been made several times to the increasingly complex nature of modern learning. Many schools and classrooms within schools are now so complex as to demand a high level of managerial skills in teachers and head teachers. In a situation which is particularly complicated managerial ability is an absolute necessity because there is so much that can go wrong. If the organisation is not highly efficient the results may be quite disastrous.

Reference has also been made to the demands that are sometimes made on teachers before they are fully equipped to cope with them. All teachers need to organise efficiently even if they are operating in a relatively simple and uncomplicated situation. A teacher who wishes to introduce more complex and fluid learning opportunities may consider it wise to do so gradually, for a variety of reasons, one of which might be in order to develop his organisational skills as he proceeds.

One of the most important points about organisation is that it exists to serve the curriculum. It was suggested in the opening paragraph that organisation should be considered *after* the curriculum has been devised. In this way it becomes the servant of the curriculum. If organisation is considered first it may exercise undesirable control over the curriculum and may become an end in itself.

The remainder of this chapter will be concerned with aspects of organisation. In some cases it will be in the form of questions which can be answered only by the teacher in relation to his own curriculum and his own situation.

TIME

How will the teacher spend his day?
How much time will he allocate to his different tasks?
How can time be arranged so that the teacher can spend a reasonable amount with each pupil?
When will the teacher do his marking?
How will the pupils' time be allocated?
Who will make decisions about this?

SPACE

Where will the different activities take place?
How can we best use the hall?
Can we use the corridors as work areas?
Is it possible to use the dining area as a work area?
How best can I divide up the classroom into work bays?

Where can I put displays, pictures, library books, materials and resources?

MOVEMENT, ACCESS AND AVAILABILITY

How best can the opportunities be organised so that pupils spend more time learning and less time moving about unnecessarily?

Is it necessary to insist on pupils keeping to the left as they walk along the school corridors?

Is it necessary to have school and class rules concerning movement? E.g. Should pupils go to the toilet only at break times?

Who is to have access to the general store cupboard?

Are pupils to be allowed to help themselves, as they need them, to paint, books, rulers, etc.?

Are pupils to be allowed, or even encouraged, to move about the classroom freely?

Is the use of certain apparatus or equipment to be restricted to older pupils?

Are pupils to be allowed to move into work areas in which teacher supervision will be only occasional or even non-existent?

When can the class or individual pupils have access to the television?

RESOURCES AND MATERIALS

The organisation should be such that resources and materials are available when and where they are needed. It will be appreciated that everything should have its place and should actually be in its place when it is required. However, it is not always appreciated that if there is a change in approach, the availability of resources and materials might have to undergo a considerable change which may be strongly resisted by some members of the staff.

This may well happen in a school in which teachers ordered and looked after their own stock. To change this so that resources and materials are generally available to all teachers in an attempt to provide wider choice and avoid duplication requires far higher organising ability. Not least among the factors to be organised will be the checking so that stock is not wasted or damaged or lost. With a system in which individual teachers look after their own stock the problem is relatively small and any failure comes back on the actual teacher concerned. This is not so when there is a general availability. It is then easy for one teacher to borrow apparatus which he forgets to return and which cannot be traced by others, for teachers to become unconcerned about materials which are not their responsibility and for aids to deteriorate. In such circumstances where the organisation does not include built-in checks to see that it is working and that all the teachers concerned are playing their parts, the pupils themselves will soon realise the position and they too may become careless. Perhaps the idea of a resource centre or even several resource centres within a school may be helpful in many situations. In this case a person or persons can be designated to be responsible, while in other schools collective responsibility may be seen as an ideal to be attempted. But, however the problem of materials and apparatus is tackled and organised there will be the need for built-in checks just as there will be a need for all teachers to be kept informed of what is available.

This chapter has considered briefly some of the factors concerned with class organisation to promote learning and has raised some of the questions which teachers are likely to have to answer. The current trend is for organisation to become more complex as schools become larger and also as teachers seek to attain an ever-widening range of objectives. The picture is further complicated by two other growing educational practices: teacher co-operation in curriculum planning and the fitting of education, as far as possible, to each individual child. The teacher, in his role of manager, has important and heavy responsibilities.

Chapter 9

Records, Evaluation and Judgement of Teaching

When a new approach to the achievement of objectives is introduced or when new objectives are selected for achievement, problems may arise concerning measurement of progress and success and the keeping of adequate records. With the kind of structured approach presented in this book, the criterion for success is the extent to which the objectives have been achieved by the pupils, provided that the approach to their achievement is morally and socially acceptable or does not produce unwanted side effects.[1] (It is assumed that the objectives themselves are desirable and acceptable and that considerable thought and care have been devoted to their selection.[2]) For example, schools will often have objectives concerned with pupils' ability to write, but not many teachers would approve of an approach to these objectives which included rapping pupils over the knuckles when they made mistakes in the hope of preventing further mistakes. Approval or disapproval of approaches on social or moral grounds may vary considerably, if not from teacher to teacher, certainly from country to country. The writers have often witnessed the approach used by swimming instructors, usually qualified teachers of physical education, to teach young children to swim at some holiday resorts in France. However nervous or frightened the children might be they are forced into the water, frequently to the accompaniment of tears or even screams. The instructors show no outward concern for their young pupils' fears and with considerable severity proceed to teach the strokes of swimming. The objective is often achieved, but the writers find the approach unacceptable on the grounds that it does not take into account the personal feelings of the child. The end does not justify the means, in our view, and we would urge teachers to consider carefully during planning all aspects of the approaches they are proposing to use, and to monitor them carefully during their actual execution.

A cyclical approach to curriculum planning assumes that the process is continuous. This gives the opportunity for constant adjustments and improvements to be made when and where necessary.

Within a structured approach of the kind advocated, teachers can more easily find evidence to suggest where these adjustments and improvements might be made and also to indicate what form they might take, but the evidence needs to be built up by the teacher in the form of carefully kept records. The idea of keeping records is not new, of course, but what may be new to some teachers is the form that the records might take. Perhaps the most common form which teachers' records usually take is that of marks or personal observations or a combination of both. The marks are likely to be those given for various pieces of work and the observations might be concerning achievement, social behaviour, appearance or attitude to work. Some records might also include scores on standardised tests.

If we are concerned with an evaluation of the curriculum which includes assessment of pupils' progress towards the objectives, records will have to be of a more comprehensive nature. It was stated above that the criterion of the success of a particular approach is the extent to which the objectives have been achieved. Suggestions have been given elsewhere[3] about the kind and form of records which might be kept of pupils' progress towards objectives, and about the ways in which this evidence can be used. Evidence of this type is likely to be numerical in form and will show the extent to which each objective has been achieved and each pupil's progress towards each objective. We might have, as a summary, a table like the one shown overleaf.

The table indicates that 76% of the pupils made progress towards objective 1, 80% towards objective 2, 84% towards objective 3, 68% towards objective 4 and 60% towards objective 5. By reading across the table we can see each pupil's record of progress. For example, pupil 1 made progress towards all five objectives while pupil 2 made progress towards only two objectives.

Evidence of this kind cannot suggest why more progress was made towards some objectives than others or why some pupils were more successful than others. Records of a different kind need to be kept to throw light on these problems and to provide information about the quality of the curriculum. Since curricula vary so much in their purposes, format and organisation, it is not possible to suggest the form that records might take, but only to indicate the range of information that might be useful in making judgements. By their nature, records of this kind will be written comments. Essentially these are observational records kept by the teacher of the curriculum in action as a check that what he planned is in fact effective. In planning a new curriculum the teacher is really putting forward a kind of practical hypothesis that it will achieve the objectives it sets out to achieve.

Summary of pupils' progress towards objectives

PUPILS	OBJECTIVES					TOTAL
	1	2	3	4	5	
1	1	1	1	1	1	5
2	1	0	0	0	1	2
3	1	1	1	1	1	5
4	1	1	1	0	0	3
5	1	1	1	1	1	5
6	0	1	0	1	0	2
7	0	1	1	1	0	3
,,						
,,						
23	1	0	1	0	1	3
24	1	1	1	1	1	5
25	0	0	1	1	1	3
	19 76%	20 80%	21 84%	17 68%	15 60%	

Note: 1=progress, 0=no progress

The hypothesis has to be tested and so evidence must be collected to support or reject it; usually, it is not a question of total acceptance or total rejection, but rather of amendment and modification which lead to another curriculum which is a further hypothesis.

The suggestions which follow concerning the range of information which might be collected for use in making amendments or changes in the curriculum are not intended to be exhaustive, since curricula of many kinds are offered in schools. It is hoped that these suggestions cover many of the common elements of various curricula and that they will encourage readers to think of others which might be relevant in particular cases.

Records might be kept concerning the level of difficulty of materials being used by the pupils. The nature of the materials is likely to vary considerably and could include books, films, filmstrips, tapes, pictures, charts, work sheets, questionnaires, assignment cards and items of equipment. However, if diagnosis was carried out adequately before the approach was planned, such records will be more in the nature of a check to ensure that the pre-selected materials and aids are in fact performing the functions they were chosen to perform and are of the appropriate level of difficulty.

It may become apparent that a curriculum is demanding and requiring of pupils' skills or knowledge which they do not have. Such a situation is likely to arouse frustration in pupils and to prevent some aspects of learning from taking place. Evidence of this kind included in records could be most valuable at the diagnosis stage when further curriculum planning is taking place. One would hope that the original diagnosis made before the designing of the curriculum under scrutiny would ensure that there is no serious mis-matching between pupils and curriculum. However, teachers in this country do not have at their disposal large batteries of standardised objective tests to help them with the task of diagnosis, and so they usually have to rely on their own tests and their own professional judgement based on their pupils' previous performance. While these might be fairly accurate in assessing the points or the levels at which pupils might begin a new curriculum, they might be less accurate in assessing the next steps, which may be more in the nature of educated guesses on the part of the teacher.

Records might also include evidence about the sequence of learning opportunities presented to pupils. It might be considered, for example, that a particular order is hindering rather than helping learning and suggestions for an alternative sequence could be included in teachers' records.

Another aspect of the learning opportunities about which teachers might comment in their records is the frequency of occasions for pupils to practise the behaviours described in the objectives. It is not uncommon for curriculum developers to underestimate the number of learning opportunities necessary for pupils to make progress towards certain kinds of objectives. This is more likely to be so in the case of high level mental skills and of emotional and social objectives.

Related to this is the level of difficulty of the objectives themselves. Teachers may feel that progress could be made towards certain objectives if more learning opportunities related to these objectives were

provided, but it might also be felt that certain objectives are too difficult. This kind of information might be included in the records.

Other information might be about the techniques of assessment of
pupils' progress towards the objectives and about the actual occasions
when assessment is to take place. In cases where 'home-made' forms
of assessment are used, especially for social and emotional objectives,
teachers may well feel that the instrument is not really capable of
assessing what it was intended to assess. Teachers' observations,
recorded at the time, could be very valuable in improving instruments
of this kind. Similarly, comments on the appropriateness of a particular occasion chosen for assessment purposes could be most helpful.
An occasion chosen for assessment purposes needs to be one which
positively evokes the behaviour which is being assessed. If it does less
than this, then assessments will be made on a false basis. Comments
recorded at the time can help to prevent this from happening.

The pupils and the teacher are the personnel involved in the curriculum and it could be useful for records to be kept of their reactions.
In the case of pupils, many of their reactions are likely to be covered
in considering the points already mentioned, but in some circumstances it may be helpful to keep separate records of pupils' reactions
and, indeed, of pupils' opinions about the curriculum. Enjoyment,
while not the main criterion of success, is an important factor worth
noting for future action. This would apply to both pupils and teachers,
as would any *undue* tension, strain or discomfort in learning opportunities.

To summarise, then, it is suggested that in evaluating an approach
to the achievement of objectives it is important to keep records of
different kinds, some of which may be numerical and formal, while
others may be verbal (written) and informal. Informal records may be
used to throw light on reasons for progress or lack of progress towards
the objectives, thus accounting to some extent for the numerical
evidence. Such informal records may be concerned with many aspects
of the curriculum, of which the following suggestions are but some:

1. level of difficulty of materials
2. prerequisite skills or knowledge
3. frequency of occasions to practise behaviours described in
   objectives
4. level of difficulty of objectives
5. techniques of assessment
6. occasions for assessment
7. reactions of pupils
8. reactions of teacher(s).

Two further points need to be made about these aspects of the curriculum. First, the evidence collected and recorded may be of a general nature and relate to the whole class, but it is far more likely to relate to particular pupils. For example, it is most unlikely that all pupils will find the materials in the curriculum of equal difficulty. The range of reading ability, for instance, may be such that some pupils will experience no difficulty with printed materials while others may experience great difficulty. Similarly, with points 2, 3, 4 and 7 listed above. If records are kept for individual pupils, where appropriate, not only do they help to provide an explanation why a pupil has made little progress towards the objectives, but they also provide information which enables the teacher to modify the approach under scrutiny to suit more appropriately the needs of particular pupils. This could mean, for example, providing simpler books, individual work cards or questionnaires, more opportunities to practise certain behaviours, individual help with particular skills and opportunity to acquire some background knowledge, or any combination of these.

The second point concerns the source of the curriculum which is being evaluated. Even if the curriculum has been designed in the school by the teacher(s) using it, records of the kind suggested should be kept. If the curriculum was planned for a particular group of pupils *on the basis of sound principles and with skill*, it may be that the evidence of the records indicates that only a few changes of a minor nature are necessary. If, however, the curriculum was designed outside the school for a generalised group of pupils, the records assume even greater importance. In order to be used effectively in a particular school with its own individuality, a curriculum designed outside is likely to have to undergo extensive modification. Curriculum modification demands the same skills and knowledge as curriculum development and can follow the same principles. Well kept and appropriate records are a valuable tool in carrying out curriculum modification of this kind.

Readers with no previous experience of keeping records of this particular kind may well feel that the task of curriculum evaluation is a formidable one in terms of time. There is no doubt that it is time-consuming and care must be taken that it does not get out of hand. Time spent on it should be justified in terms of curriculum improvement. Record keeping is a means to an end and not an end in itself.

So far in this chapter we have been concerned with aspects of judgements about the success of curricula. Not infrequently, such judgements are based on general impressions or generalised opinions with little or no factual evidence to support these. Until we have accurate and reliable assessment techniques to measure pupils' progress towards all the objectives we wish them to pursue, curriculum evaluation cannot be a completely scientific process. However, it can be more scientific than if general impressions or generalised opinions are the only criteria and the keeping of records along the lines suggested is a step, albeit a small one, in the direction of deeper understanding and greater precision.

Judgements are also frequently made about teaching ability: judgements about students on teaching practice, about qualified teachers by inspectors, head teachers, colleagues, parents and pupils. Criteria for success are frequently unstated and judgements are often made on the basis of a general impression, sometimes gained during a short period of time. Among the criteria likely to be used are the teacher's (or student's) ability to establish good order in the classroom, to maintain reasonable relationships with pupils, to keep the pupils' attention and interest, to keep the pupils busy, and to act confidently in the classroom.

It is too easy to make instant and superficial judgements of whether teaching *looks* impressive or whether the pupils are working happily and well. Professional teachers deserve to be judged against a more soundly-based criteria than these. A teacher is trained in both theory and practice and it is suggested that his training should equip him to do the following:

1. identify and justify appropriate aims and objectives for his pupils
2. identify and use factors in the situation which affect the curriculum
3. create approaches to aims and objectives which provide opportunities for all pupils to make progress
4. modify approaches on the basis of feedback from the curriculum in action
5. assess pupils' progress towards the objectives.

These objectives then provide criteria against which teaching ability can be judged. In making judgements it is important to know first what a teacher is trying to achieve. Any criticism or praise is then given, either in terms of the appropriateness of his aims and objectives, or in terms of his efforts to achieve them. Questions which might be considered by those wishing to make judgements of teaching could include the following:

1. Are the aims/objectives stated explicitly as well as implicitly in the activity going on?
2. Are the explicit and implicit aims/objectives closely related?
3. Is the range of aims appropriate—not too wide or too narrow?
4. Do all pupils stand a reasonable chance of progressing towards the objectives?
5. Does the balance of pupil activity reflect the relative importance attached by the teacher to various objectives?
6. Are there likely to be any unwanted side-effects from the pupils' activity? (i.e. are any unwanted objectives being achieved?)
7. Are the aims, objectives, learning opportunities and assessment techniques consistent with each other?

In order to answer questions such as these, evidence would have to be sought from teachers' record books, from discussions and from observation of the activity in the classroom. It is sometimes said that teachers resent or fear judgements of their teaching. It is perfectly understandable that this should be so if the judgements are made on the basis of vague and often unstated criteria. If judgements are made on the basis of whether a teacher uses 'modern methods' (whatever these are), or whether what he and the pupils are doing *looks* good, or whether the pupils' exercise books look neat, or, what is perhaps worse, on the basis of unspoken criteria, then teachers are justified in their resentment of judgements being made. If, however, judgements are made on the basis of clearly-stated criteria which make professional sense to teachers, then those who take their work seriously and take pride in it are unlikely to show opposition or resentment. Indeed, most of us wish to know whether we are being successful and efficient in our work and would welcome a sound basis for knowing this.

NOTES

1 Readers who are not familiar with this notion of assessment should read S. Wiseman and D. Pidgeon, *Curriculum Evaluation* (NFER, 1970), and A. and H. Nicholls, *Developing a Curriculum* (Allen & Unwin, 1972), Ch. 6.
2 See A. and H. Nicholls, op. cit., pp. 35–8 and R. W. Tyler, *Basic Principles of Curriculum and Instruction* (University of Chicago Press, 1969), pp. 5–43.
3 A. and H. Nicholls, op. cit., pp. 80–4.

Chapter 10

Implementing Innovations

The earlier chapters in this book have been concerned in various ways with the planning and creating of approaches for the achievement of particular desired objectives. A school staff which is actively involved in curriculum planning over a period of years is likely to be concerned mainly with approaches which differ only slightly from those previously tried and sometimes, less frequently, with approaches which differ considerably from previous ones. Such markedly different approaches can be said to constitute innovations for the teachers concerned and might take the form of new courses, new forms of organisation (e.g. non-streaming) or new teaching procedures (e.g. team teaching), or, indeed, any combination of these.

It will be apparent to the reader that curriculum development is a complex activity requiring knowledge and skills of a high order, as well as considerable time and a variety of resources. However, if such professional expertise and effort are not to be wasted some careful attention should be given to the period between the development of an innovation (as defined above) and its actual implementation. We can consider as an example the situation in which a group of teachers, encouraged and supported by their head, have worked together and developed a new course for a particular year of pupils. The intention is that the course should be introduced into the school at the beginning of the new school year by the teacher-developers. In this situation the teachers are likely to be favourably disposed to the innovation (although, of course, this would not be the case with all innovations), but during the school year all kinds of unforeseen difficulties arise connected with the innovation and by the middle of the year none of the teachers is using it; in other words, the innovation has not been implemented by any of the teachers. Successful implementation might go along these lines: teachers have an idea for a new approach to the achievement of their objectives which they then plan using normal curriculum development procedures. The new approach is introduced to the pupils concerned and tried out over a period of time, during which it might be modified on the basis of feedback from the situation. Only when the approach is fully operational can it be said that the innovation has been implemented, as is shown in the figure below.

Stages leading to implementation of an innovation.

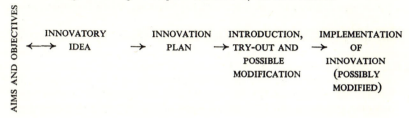

Unfortunately, the period between the development of an innovation plan and its implementation is seldom given close attention inside the school and this sometimes leads to frustration and disappointment when innovations are not fully or even partly implemented. The purpose of this chapter is to examine the conditions and actions which are likely to facilitate the implementation of educationl innovations.[1]

If an individual teacher develops an innovation of his own which he wishes to introduce to his pupils and the innovation does not involve or directly affect any other members of staff, this represents a comparatively simple and uncomplicated situation in terms of implementation. Even so, problems may be present or arise in a situation as straightforward as this. Some factors in the situation would be conducive to a successful implementation of the innovation. The teacher would be favourably disposed towards the innovation since it is by his own choice that he wishes to use it. It is of his own creation and one would therefore expect that he would understand it and that it was within his capabilities to cope with it. From where then might factors arise which might cause problems related to its implementation?

Some such factors are under the control of the head teacher. These would include time, money, resources and administrative or organisational arrangements. If, for example, an innovation requires blocked periods on the timetable and the head cannot or will not provide these, it cannot be fully implemented. If more space is required and this cannot be provided, again, full implementation will not occur. The implications here for the innovating teacher are for full discussions and consultations with the head teacher both before and during planning so that all the factors relevant to the innovation are made clear in order that disappointment and frustration are not brought about on this count.

The school staff, even though they are not directly affected by or involved with the innovation, may be a source of factors which could lead to the ultimate rejection of an individual teacher's innovation.

These could arise particularly if the innovation deviates greatly from the acceped norm in the school. Other teachers might feel threatened by it or might see it as an implied criticism of what they themselves are doing. This could lead to open criticism of the innovation (and/or of the teacher involved) to such an extent that the innovator may feel compelled to discard it. Such criticisms might vary in their extent, severity and direction according to the power and/or prestige of the innovating teacher within the school staff. What might a teacher do to avoid arousing the fears or antagonism of his colleagues? There is no clear and simple answer to this question, since so much depends on the particular situation, but whatever the situation he would be wise to keep his colleagues as fully informed as possible of his plans and to give them opportunities to question him about what he is doing. He should reassure them, as well as he can, about any fears they may have. Two-way communication would appear to be very important. The innovator should remember that even an individual teacher's innovation might well affect his colleagues, at least indirectly. If the innovating teacher is in a position of low power and prestige in the staff, he may find it helpful to win for his innovation the support of a member of the staff with high prestige, who could then put his case to the staff with greater effect.

Another possible source of factors which might operate against successful implementation are the pupils for whom the innovation is intended. Opposition might be open and direct in the sense that the pupils simply do not wish the innovation to become operative, but this is less likely than more indirect forms of opposition. It may be, for example, that the innovation is making demands on the pupils to which they are not able to respond; these might be demands of prerequisite skills or knowledge which they do not have. It might involve ways of working which are unfamiliar to them, or be concerned with knowledge and ideas which are too difficult or which they cannot see as relevant. If a situation arises for reasons like those just cited the teacher may have developed his innovation without adequate or sufficiently accurate diagnosis of the pupils for whom it is intended. In addition to carrying out a diagnosis before undertaking development work, teachers might find it helpful to communicate to their pupils information about the innovation so that pupils will know what purposes it serves and what is expected of them. Pupils are often as conservative as some teachers, perhaps for similar reasons. It may be necessary to resolve their fears, change their attitudes and seek their co-operation, as well as simply to provide them with information.

The comparatively simple and uncomplicated situation just outlined of an individual teacher wishing to introduce an innovation of his own creation which does not involve or directly affect his colleagues is one which rarely exists. Firstly, as we have already seen, few innovations in education are entirely of a teacher's own creation, but also most innovations affect and involve several if not all members of staff. This means that in reality most situations involving innovations are far more complex than that just described and the problems which can be associated with implementation may be greater, more complex and more numerous.

The suggestion to introduce an innovation into a school may come from the head, or an individual or a group of teachers, who will first have to convince the head that the idea is at least worth a trial. At some stage it is likely that other teachers will have to be persuaded that the innovation is worthwhile and their co-operation and participation sought. The doubts and fears mentioned above, in the case of the colleagues of the individual innovating teacher, may be present in this situation, but they could be more strongly felt since active co-operation and participation are being sought. The greater the differences between the innovation and what the teachers are accustomed to, the greater may be their doubts and fears. Teachers who are not constantly introducing innovations or enthusiastically supporting the innovations of their colleagues are frequently criticised and called 'traditional', a term used in a derogatory sense. Potential innovators might look a little more carefully and a little more sympathetically at the doubts expressed by their colleagues. In the first place it is not unnatural that doubts should be expressed. A teacher proceeding in a particular way is likely to feel secure in what he is doing and confident in his ability to do it. If he is suddenly asked to make fundamental changes, he may feel that his security is threatened and he may genuinely doubt his ability to carry out the innovation. He may express these fears as criticisms of the innovation itself. It is unlikely that teachers will admit openly doubts about their ability to carry out innovations in some schools, since such expressions may well be interpreted as admissions of professional incompetency and may be damaging to the careers of the teachers concerned. Innovators, therefore, need to be sensitive to the possible reasons underlying criticisms and comments about their proposals and need to be sympathetic and tactful in dealing with them. Moreover, the expression of doubts and criticisms may serve a very useful purpose in forcing an enthusiastic innovator to support his ideas with convincing arguments and this may lead to clearer thinking on his own part about the innovation.

Intending innovators need to recognise the importance of adequate channels of communication within a school and to ensure that the channels are used. It needs to be recognised also that this step of creating interest and winning support may well take quite a long time. Attitudes tend not to change quickly and frequent opportunities need to be provided for discussions among those involved. This perhaps calls for planning over a longer period of time than is usual in schools, but too frequently *ad hoc* arrangements are made or plans drawn up on a short-term basis and these often have disappointing results.

The innovators need to bear in mind that, in terms of the innovation they are proposing, they are likely to be further ahead than their colleagues in their thinking and also in their feelings about the innovation, and that they themselves may well have had a considerable length of time to reach their present stage. Colleagues should also be given time to consider fully what they are being asked to do. Time devoted to this stage is likely to pay dividends in the end. Teachers who are pressurised into going along with an innovation may outwardly support it, but in reality the innovation may not be implemented by them. The innovators also have a responsibility to ensure that the nature and implications of the innovation are made absolutely clear to those who will be involved. If participating teachers do not have a clear picture of the innovation there is no possibility of its being implemented in its original form [2].

It was mentioned earlier that one of the doubts which teachers might have about an innovation is their ability to cope with it. Some innovations may indeed require skills, expertise or knowledge which some teachers do not have, and to introduce an innovation of this kind without making any necessary provision for them to acquire that which is lacking is extremely unwise, to say the least. One can think of several major innovations being introduced at the present time which may necessitate a rather drastic change in the role of the teacher: the open-plan design of primary schools, non-streaming, vertical grouping, Stenhouse's Humanities Project. Are teachers always given the opportunity for in-service education to help them cope with these new situations? We fear not. Again, time is an important factor. Innovators tend to want to make changes quickly and yet their innovation might be better served by a little less haste, so that any necessary staff training can be carried out.

The role of the head teacher is a crucial one in the successful acceptance and implementation of innovations. Frequent reference has been made in this chapter to the need for time—time for discussion, time for thinking, time for persuasion, time for further education.

While it is unrealistic and possibly unreasonable to expect that all these activities should take place during school time, it is equally unrealistic and unreasonable that they should all take place after school. It is the head who can ensure that some time is allocated during the working day to the types of activity mentioned.

The head can also control, to some extent, the conflict which can arise between the desire of the innovator to proceed quickly and the necessity of allowing time for colleagues to become convinced and retrained where necessary. If it is the head himself who is the innovator he needs to recognise the need to strike an appropriate balance between these somewhat conflicting demands. In the interests of progress, as he sees it, it is more than likely that he may decide to proceed before everyone can possibly become convinced or trained. In this case, he has the responsibility of ensuring that the work of changing attitudes and providing in-service education continues after the innovation has been introduced.

The role of the head is also vital in that it is he who can provide or acquire resources which the innovation needs and he who can set up the appropriate conditions for it to proceed. Resources here might include time, money, space and equipment. The appropriate conditions could include allocation of pupils, staff, aides and groupings of pupils. Teachers presenting proposals for innovations to their head teachers have a responsibility to make clear, as well as they are able, the kind of resources and conditions the innovation is likely to require, just as head teachers have a responsibility to ensure that they are able to provide these before an attempt is made to introduce the innovation or to begin work on it, whichever the case may be.

It is a fairly widespread view in educational circles that it is 'a good thing' to have innovations in schools. In this climate of opinion it is understandable that head teachers should be willing and possibly even anxious to introduce innovations into their schools because of the prestige that this may give them. This attitude could lead to a situation in which innovations are introduced without full consideration being given to the implications of such actions. For example, are its objectives compatible with those of the school? Does it require resources the school cannot provide? Will it make too heavy demands on the staff? A further possible difficulty may come from the fact that it is not always realised that there is a big difference between the initial introduction of an innovation and its eventual full implementation. For example, it may be decided (or even agreed) to destream and this might actually be carried out in administrative and organisational terms. If, however, some teachers continue to stream within the class, this innovation has not been implemented. Much effort, energy and time might have to be spent by those convinced of the desirability of certain innovations for implementation to occur. This might be the case even when teachers are involved in decision-making and in actual development work. Difficulties might arise for some teachers which they are not able to cope with without help and they might be unwilling to ask for this. In some cases, the implications of the innovation might not have been made clear to them at the outset and so they are unable to implement it [3]. Innovators have a responsibility to provide a form of school-based in-service education wherever and whenever this might be needed. It might be necessary during all stages in the life of an innovation: during development work (and even before development work begins), at the stage of introduction and following introduction until the innovation is implemented. An innovation might be compared to a rather delicate plant. If it is to take root and flourish, much previous attention must be given to the soil and loving care given to the plant itself. If these conditions are not fulfilled, it will wither and die. It is, of course, not only head teachers who need to be aware of these factors. Teachers should also realise the implications of introducing an innovation, and this calls for a thorough understanding of the innovation itself as well as knowledge of the conditions under which a successful implementation is likely to occur.

In some situations, such as the appointment of a new head teacher or the reorganisation of a school or moving into a new building, there is a tendency for innovation on a wide scale to be attempted. This is understandable, for such situations seem to offer an ideal opportunity, if not for a fresh start, at least for widespread change. While it is acknowledged that some schools are well able to cope fully with considerable change, one must question the wisdom of attempting this in all cases. Those who are anxious to promote change should bear in mind the complex nature of the tasks of both developing and implementing educational innovations. They should consider most carefully the ability of the staff in relation to these tasks and they should analyse the conditions in the school in terms of their suitability to foster change on a wide scale. Taking into account the points made previously, concerning the difference between the initial introduction and the full implementation of an innovation, and realising that some complex innovations might require a considerable length of time before they are fully implemented, it might prove to be more fruitful in the long run to ensure that innovations are being implemented before new ones are introduced. Much depends, of course, on the conditions in each individual school: the experience of the staff in implementing innovations, the pupils for whom the innovations are intended, the size of the school and so on. The decisions about rate of change can only be taken in individual schools in the light of existing circumstances, but it is suggested that the points just mentioned might profitably be among those which are considered.

The main points in this chapter have been to indicate the gap that can exist between the introduction of an innovatory idea into a school and the eventual implementation of an innovation. Much of what has been written may appear to the reader as self-evident and just plain common sense. This may be so, and yet one reads in the literature [4] and finds in one's own experience cases where innovations are not being implemented, partly, at least, because of a disregard for some or all of the factors mentioned in this chapter. It may well be that we are aware of these factors at the intellectual level but unless we step back and really think about them in relation to what is going on in school we tend not to put them into practice.

The factors which are considered to be conducive to the successful implementation of innovation and which have been discussed in this chapter are summarised and listed below.

FACTORS CONDUCIVE TO SUCCESSFUL IMPLEMENTATION
OF INNOVATIONS

1. Teachers are favourably disposed towards innovation.
2. Teachers have clear understanding of innovation.
3. Innovation is within teachers' capabilities.
4. Necessary resources for innovation are provided.
5. Necessary administrative/organisational arrangements are made.
6. Full and accurate pupil diagnosis is carried out.
7. Channels of communication are used for: (a) giving information; (b) seeking co-operation; (c) resolving fears; (d) changing attitudes.
8. In-service education is available where necessary in connection with factors 2, 3, 6 and 7.
9. Adequate time is given for development of factors 1, 2, 3, 6, 7 and 8.

To illustrate how these factors might operate in a school an example is offered concerning a headmaster who wishes to introduce non-streaming in his school. It must be emphasised that the example is not intended to suggest that this is *the* way innovations or even this particular innovation should be introduced and nurtured. It is merely an example to illustrate the points discussed in the chapter.

EXAMPLE TO ILLUSTRATE APPLICATION OF FACTORS LEADING
TO THE SUCCESSFUL IMPLEMENTATION OF AN INNOVATION

At the end of an academic year when reflecting on pupils' progress
towards the school's aims and objectives the head teacher is less than
satisfied with some aspects of pupil development. Some pupils display
negative attitudes to school, while others have low levels of aspiration
and poor self-images. Little progress appears to have been made
towards improving personal relationships, both among pupils and
between pupils and staff. In view of this, the head teacher decides that
he would like to re-organise the school on the basis of non-streaming.
He is aware that research on the relative merits of streamed and
unstreamed classes is inconclusive but that it does suggest that there
is little or no difference in academic achievement providing teachers
are in favour of the form of organisation and use appropriate teaching
methods. Research indicates that there may be some social, emotional
and attitudinal benefits to be derived from an unstreamed organisation, again, if teachers have positive attitudes towards it.

At the beginning of the new academic year the head takes the first
steps towards putting his idea into operation. He calls together his
senior members of staff to discuss the idea and the reasons behind it
and some of the practical implications of putting it into practice. The
senior teachers agree with the head that the idea is a good one and
that it is possible at the practical level. The head and senior staff then
talk informally to individual and small groups of teachers about the
nature of the change being contemplated and reassure them that no
decisions will finally be taken until the staff have been consulted and
given the opportunity to seek further information and to express their
views.

During the course of a number of further discussions with senior
staff the head ensures that they fully understand the ways in which
non-streaming is likely to affect teacher roles, relationships, teaching
approaches, record keeping and assessment, use of materials and aids,
etc. He checks how many of the senior staff have the necessary knowledge and expertise to help him guide other teachers who are not
familiar with the problems of dealing with pupils with particularly
wide ranges of abilities, attitudes, interests and so on. For those senior
staff without this knowledge and expertise, arrangements are made for
visits to other schools, for visiting speakers and for attendance at in-
service courses, and suggestions are made for appropriate reading. The
head decides to continue discussions with his senior staff to clarify
their perceptions of the innovation, to share their joint expertise and

knowledge and to prepare them to help their colleagues more ably at a later date.

In the meantime, he and his senior colleagues check on the availability of the materials, equipment and aids which they consider to be necessary for the new form of organisation. Deficiences are noted and provision is made for these to be supplied should the innovation be approved, together with any other items which may prove to be necessary.

When they are sure that all members of staff have been given information about the proposed innovation on an informal basis, the head and senior staff agree that it is time to call together the whole staff to discuss the idea more fully with them. A number of meetings are held during which the proposal is made, staff are encouraged to give their opinions and discussions are held. Among the topics discussed are: the nature of the innovation and its justification in terms of the school's aims and objectives; the practical implications of the innovation and areas of difficulty that can be anticipated; the arrangements for guidance and support for teachers who need it from the head and his senior colleagues and for other forms of in-service education where necessary; how the success of the innovation will be judged; and arrangements for lines of communication through which teachers, children and head teacher can give and receive information.

At a meeting held during the first week of the spring term the decision is taken following a majority vote by the teachers not to stream in the first year from the beginning of the next academic year. If this proves to be successful in promoting the social, emotional and attitudinal aims desired by the staff, non-streaming will be extended from the following year. The spring and summer terms are to be spent in making the necessary preparations.

During these two terms many discussions take place and a number of working parties are set up. In-service courses are held in school, while individual teachers visit other schools and attend outside in-service activities. Visits are made to the contributing schools to gather information about the pupils who will be involved in the innovation. The teachers who will be directly involved work together to plan new learning opportunities for the pupils. Work is started on the development of techniques to assess progress towards the desired objectives. From time to time full staff meetings are held, progress reports given and problems and difficulties discussed.

At the beginning of the following year the first year forms are organised on an unstreamed basis, the procedure being fully explained to the new pupils by the head teacher. During this year he and his senior colleagues keep in close touch with the teachers directly involved in the innovation, providing support and guidance when unforeseen problems arise and arranging for further in-service education when this proves necessary. The teachers concerned are constantly on the alert for difficulties experienced by the pupils and are aware of the need to modify their planned learning opportunities in the light of feedback from the situation. Throughout the year both informal and formal meetings take place to discuss the innovation. On some occasions these are between the head and the staff involved and on others they include the whole staff.

By the end of the spring term the general view of the staff is that the innovation is proving successful and this general assessment is supported by the more formal assessment carried out, using techniques to assess progress towards the objectives. This encourages the staff to reaffirm their decision to extend non-streaming and for those who are to be involved to begin planning.

Support and encouragement for the original group of innovating teachers continues during the summer term, while the second group is given opportunities for discussion, in-service functions of various types and the general kind of assistance and facilities which their colleagues had the previous year. The original group of teachers help their colleagues considerably in these activities.

At the end of the summer term the teachers involved with the first year unstreamed groups present their report to their colleagues. They report that while class teaching has not been entirely eliminated by all of them the emphasis during the year has been on individual and group work, the groups being made up in a number of ways according to the particular objectives they were pursuing. They feel that they still have much to learn about working in this way and about producing materials for a wide range of abilities, but they believe that a satisfactory start has been made. The assessment procedures show a continuance of the progress towards the objectives reported the previous term and this is considered to be satisfactory progress. The head teacher is satisfied that as far as the first year pupils are concerned the innovation has been implemented.

NOTES

1 The observations which follow in this chapter apply to both innovations developed inside the school and to those developed outside (e.g. by the Schools Council).

2 See N. Gross, J. B. Giacquinta and M. Bernstein, *Implementing Organisational Innovations* (Harper & Row, 1971).

3 Gross, *et al.,* op. cit.

4 Gross, *et al.,* op. cit.; M. Shipman, *Inside a Curriculum Project* (Methuen, 1974).

Chapter 11

Conclusion

It was stated in the opening chapter that the basic idea which runs through this book is that change is more likely to be effective and justifiable when it is carefully planned with clear and reasonable purposes in mind and when the curricula thus devised reflect what is practically possible and not just theoretically desirable. As new teachers come into the profession and as existing teachers learn more and develop new ideas, so educational practice is constantly changing. The changes which teachers seek to introduce into schools reflect their efforts to improve in some way the education they are offering to their pupils.

Stated briefly and simply, the teacher's task, as we see it, is to further the progress of all pupils towards ends which are largely previously determined. However simply this task may be stated it is very difficult to carry out. A teacher's work is of a highly complex nature which requires considerable knowledge, a wide variety of skills and positive attitudes. We have attempted to show in this book that the teacher needs a model on which to base his curriculum planning. The one suggested here requires that he has a sound knowledge of the basic disciplines of education in order to analyse his situation, select appropriate aims and objectives, devise related learning opportunities and assess his pupil's progress. He needs knowledge and expertise to guide him through a whole range of decisions he has to make, whether these are concerned with grouping, use of aids, forms of organisation or ways to implement his new curriculum.

A recent trend in some schools is towards joint curriculum planning. In our view this is usually a highly desirable state of affairs not only because of the benefits of the pooling and sharing of knowledge, ideas and expertise, but also because a curriculum so created is more likely to be consistent and unified. It needs to be recognised, however, that co-operative planning demands its own expertise in the areas of personal relationships and group functioning. An interesting point here is that teachers who carry out curriculum planning in a group frequently derive from this experience insights into and experience of personal relationships and the workings of groups which they then use to good effect with their pupils.

Some teachers may fear that working with colleagues in this way might result in a diminution of their personal autonomy. It is true that compromise positions may sometimes have to be reached and that individual viewpoints may have to be modified in the interests of a unified and consistent curriculum, but within this approach there is considerable opportunity for individuality on the part of each teacher. It permits teachers both to plan and function as individuals within a generally agreed framework. Moreover, although a teacher may give up some of his autonomy by working in this way, he also is able to exert some influence over the work of his colleagues.

The notion of individuality is very important and has been stressed in this book. Teachers are unique individuals and as such should be permitted to express their individuality. This is not to say that every teacher must be allowed to do what he wants, when he wants and how he wants. It is to say that all teachers should not be expected to think exactly the same or to work in exactly the same way. They are usually expected to work within a commonly accepted framework, if only because of the demands of society in general and of individual interests within it.

Just as teachers are unique individuals so too are pupils. The ideal that has been advocated has been for a curriculum created and adapted to the individual needs, attainments, potentialities and interests of each pupil. It is recognised that, for the most part, this can be only an ideal since realism demands that the practicalities of the situation must be taken into account and these rarely permit a completely individualised curriculum for every pupil. However, it is no bad thing to strive towards an ideal since from striving can come progress.

Another aspect of individuality which needs to be taken into account is that of the situation in which teachers and pupils are to operate and of which they are a part. There may be many features which situations have in common but there are also many differences. This being so, although learning opportunities devised by particular teachers for their particular pupils in their particular situation may have some similarities with others devised by other teachers for other pupils elsewhere, they have also their unique features. Thus, taking into account these various aspects of individuality, there are no 'right' answers and no 'right' ways of proceeding that can be applied to all situations or transferred from one situation to another.

Although this book is concerned with educational change, it does not advocate change simply for its own sake. It is concerned with planned and purposeful change to bring about improved learning. The teacher who is constantly changing according to every educational fashion or fancy, and who does not allow time for evaluation, for full implementation or for pupils to progress in the desired direction, can be a menace to both his pupils and his colleagues. A menace of a different kind is the teacher who thinks he has found the 'right' answer and who no longer questions what he is doing. Teachers of this kind may include those who are sometimes labelled 'progressive' or 'modern' as well as those sometimes labelled 'traditional' or 'old-fashioned'. There is as much stagnation when a teacher *always* uses sub-groups, teaches his pupils and arranges his furniture in a particular informal way as when a teacher *always* teaches his class as one group and arranges his desks in rows. It is important to achieve a balance somewhere between constant change and stagnation. Where that balance lies will depend on the circumstances in each particular situation, as will the nature and extent of the change.

Little has been said about parents. In a situation where educational ideas and practice are changing, parents may become worried and confused, and what may begin as lack of understanding may become lack of sympathy or even antagonism. Parents' own experience of education is likely to be very different from that of their children. In order to secure the co-operation of parents, teachers must first ensure that parents understand what they are trying to do, how they are doing it and why they are doing it. In cases where parents are particularly articulate they may also be expected to justify what they are doing. It has already been suggested that such explanations will come more easily if teachers have planned their curriculum on a rational basis.

The complex nature of present-day education means that the work of a teacher is no longer simply that of an instructor. His work now has many facets. At different times he may be operating as a guide, a motivator, a facilitator, an organiser, a manager, a model, a resource, a planner, a developer, an assessor or evaluator, a counsellor, a consultant, as well as an instructor. However complicated and demanding his work may be, it is also challenging and rewarding. Its ever-changing nature makes it interesting, varied, and at times, when plans are being made and hypotheses tested, quite exciting.

The concept of creative teaching with which this book has been concerned is that of a profession in which its members have the appropriate knowledge, skills, expertise and attitudes to participate in decision-making of many kinds and to devise learning opportunities which will further the maximum learning of all their pupils.

Appendix A :

Some 'Difficult' Objectives

It was stated in Chapter 2 (page 27) that some objectives are not easy to achieve and often require the concerted efforts of a whole staff over a long period of time. This often applies to affective and high level cognitive objectives. Newly qualified teachers have not had the opportunity to acquire the considerable professional expertise which is necessary to help pupils progress towards such objectives.

In this appendix examples will be given of objectives which experience has shown can present problems. Suggestions will be made about what teachers and pupils might do to further the achievement of these objectives and about the kind of difficulties which might be associated with them.

It should be stressed that these suggestions are only examples and that there are more ways than are suggested here of achieving these objectives. Equally, the opportunities exemplified could also be used to achieve additional objectives to those quoted.

Example 1

Aim: to develop sympathetic attitudes towards the needs and welfare of others.

This is usually an over-arching school aim and lends itself to being broken down in a variety of ways for different age groups and in different areas of the curriculum. This aim is frequently at the heart of many social studies courses for older secondary pupils, particularly courses which include a compulsory element of community service.

Objectives derived from the above aim for part of such a course might include the following:

1. shows concern for the welfare of others
2. displays tolerance of differences among people
3. demonstrates commitment to social improvement
4. volunteers for special social tasks to be undertaken in his own time.

Some form of community work provides a suitable opportunity for the achievement of these objectives, but it must be stated most emphatically that participation in community work of itself will not necessarily ensure progress towards the objectives. First, it must be recognised that community work in this situation is not on a voluntary basis since it forms an integral part of a school course. Only when pupils act voluntarily is it evidence of the qualities indicated in the general aim. The hope in the school situation is that the experiences the pupils undergo in the social studies course will lead to instances of these developing sympathetic attitudes, as can be seen from objectives 3 and 4.

Moreover, the undertaking of community work will not automatically lead to the concern and tolerance desired by objectives 1 and 2. For example, pupils visiting the home of an old person who is constantly criticising young people in general and their efforts in particular may develop most intolerant attitudes to old people because they do not understand the problems of the old person. Similarly, with old persons who constantly say they do not require or want any help, or who insist on things being done their way, or who will not stop talking and keep on repeating themselves, pupils not understanding the underlying reasons for this behaviour, may in fact develop unsympathetic attitudes and be unwilling to commit themselves to any further action on behalf of old people in the community.

One way of trying to prevent difficulties of this kind, in the example just quoted, would be to invite a social worker with experience of dealing with old people to talk to the pupils *before* they begin their work. The social worker, in talking about her own experiences, would give the pupils some understanding of the behaviour of old people and prepare them for what they themselves might experience, and at the same time alert the teacher to some possible areas of difficulty. In addition, once the community work starts provision needs to be made for follow-up work in the form of discussions about what has actually happened. Discussions of this kind provide the teacher with opportunities to interpret incidents and behaviour, and also supply background information which can help him to structure future learning opportunities which will further the objectives, and, on appropriate occasions, offer one source of assessment of progress.

Community service is not always carried out on behalf of old persons, but may be connected with young children, handicapped persons or other groups. Work with different sections of the community would raise its own problems. The general point being made that work of this kind does not *automatically* lead to the achievement of objectives of the kind illustrated, also applies to these other forms of community service. There is a need for preparatory and follow-up work, a need to anticipate possible undesirable side-effects and a need to make on-going and final checks on progress towards the desired objectives.

Example 2

Aim: To encourage pupils to make choices based on their stated values and rational judgements.

As with the aim in Example 1, this is usually a school-wide aim, and indeed it may be considered to be an appropriate aim for the whole period of education. One of the major difficulties connected with this aim concerns the latter part of it: 'based on their stated rational judgements and values'. From the infant school onwards pupils are given frequent opportunities to make choices from a range of activities or courses which are available, but how often are they asked to give reasons for their choice? It is comparatively easy to make a choice, say between whether to spend a morning painting or reading an interesting book, but it is not so easy to justify the particular choice that is made. Yet, if one of the purposes of education is to help pupils to make what for them are wise choices and to realise the implications of the choices they make, they should be given appropriate learning opportunities to develop the skills involved in this. Like many other worth-while aims a great deal of time needs to be devoted to the learning opportunities associated with it, but this does not necessarily mean that *each* time *every* pupil makes a choice he should justify it.

The long-term nature of this aim suggests that careful school-wide planning needs to be undertaken so that active co-operation of the whole staff can be obtained in its pursuit. Some kind of progression needs to be planned and at the secondary stage this might be, for example, from choice of 'best buys' in groceries and choice of convenience foods *v.* traditional foods in a social studies and/or home economics course, to choice of subjects and courses, with implications for future careers, to a choice of courses of action in moral/social situations.

The 'consumer' type work provides opportunities for choices to be made on the basis of actual evidence, i.e. weight, money, time, efficiency, and so on. Pupils can support their choice with 'concrete' reasons but there is also room for them to state personal preferences. Situations of this kind can provide a starting-point at the secondary level for pupils to begin to offer reasons for making a particular choice.

Towards the end of the third year when pupils in many secondary schools are asked to make choices about the subjects and courses they will follow for the next two or more years, we have an excellent opportunity for the furtherance of this aim. The choices to be made are less 'concrete' in nature and have greater implications for the pupils' future than the consumer decisions. If pupils are to make their choices wisely with an awareness of the long-term future implications associated with their choices, they need to have had many previous experiences of basing their choices on considered judgements and values. The consumer situation is just one example of what might happen in the early years of secondary education.

If the choice of subjects and courses is to be used as valuable learning experience and at the same time to provide an opportunity for pupils to put into practice their previous relevant learning, it cannot be hurried. Teachers involved in this work need to be prepared to question their pupils patiently and to discuss the implications of their choices with them. It is a situation in which the teacher might act as a sounding-board rather than one in which they give their pupils direct answers.

A further progression with this aim might take place when pupils discuss social and moral issues where they are asked to suggest possible courses of action which might be taken. These could involve issues concerning the pupils themselves, or hypothetical characters or they might be issues of concern to society in general. We are dealing here largely in the realm of values, an area in which some pupils might have difficulty in expressing their ideas, and again, one to which a considerable amount of time might have to be devoted. Among the techniques which might be used here are small group discussion, class discussion, role-playing, written reports, drama and debates.

There are two points to be stressed with this aim. First, there is the important matter that pupils should offer reasons for the choices they make and that the reasons are based on their judgments and values. Secondly, there is the long-term nature of this aim for most pupils. The skills involved need to be analysed carefully and learning opportunities devised which, over a period of time, will help to develop them.

Example 3

Aim: to develop the ability to bring together for use information, materials and resources from a variety of sources.

This is another popular school-wide aim. There appear to be two main problems concerned with its achievement. There is the problem, probably caused by an absence of school-wide planning, of ensuring some kind of progression in the objectives connected with the aim and there is the problem of getting pupils to present their findings in a form other than that taken directly from their sources. Both difficulties can be overcome to some extent by a careful statement of objectives and by joint planning. Following this, teachers need to offer help and guidance to individual pupils to assist progress towards the stated objectives.

In this example, the aim is broken down into a number of geography objectives with a list of possible sources. The objectives are intended to be progressive and it is suggested that they might be appropriate for either individuals or groups of pupils over the period of junior and secondary education.

Objectives for individuals or groups	*Sources*
Locates information about raising cows in Britain	Class textbook.
Selects from general books on Norway, Egypt and the West Indies facts concerned with the weather.	Three books from the school library.
Makes notes using only one side of a postcard for a five-minute talk on how the map of Africa has changed since World War II.	Class, school and town libraries.
Selects and lists geographical facts common to countries or parts of countries which have a Mediterranean climate.	Books, maps, magazines in libraries. Interviews with people from two such parts of the world.
Lists and classifies sources of geographical information and the nature of that information.	Own knowledge, other people's knowledge, tables of content, catalogues, encyclopedias, embassies, National Coal Board, private industry, books, newspapers, etc.
Compiles comparative lists of information concerning the imports and exports of Britain and Nigeria.	Shipping lines, Nigerian Embassy, Libraries, Government agencies concerned with trade, books on economic geography, British and Nigerian agencies associated with production.

Objectives for individuals or groups	*Sources*
Selects from a variety of sources information concerning the possible effects of temperature on the design of houses.	Books of plans, information from embassies, holiday snapshots taken in Spain, Norway and Britain. Temperatures taken in a room with a large window area facing south at midday during a heatwave when the curtains have been closed all day and later when those curtains have been open for an hour. Libraries etc.
Paraphrases information concerning the changing nature of land utilisation in agricultural areas of Britain.	Text or reference books from the public library.
Collects information, materials and resources about the economic pros and cons of joining the Common Market with a view to a visual presentation of the results.	Selection of sources generally left to the imagination and drive of the pupil, apart from a stipulated interview schedule to be prepared and given to the class as a whole and to a stratified random sample of the population of the town.

The Progressive Interpretation of Aims

It was suggested in Chapter 2 that some aims might be considered desirable for the whole period of education. In this case, the aims would have to be interpreted and stated as objectives which were appropriate for pupils at different stages of their education. The three aims illustrated in Appendix A will be broken down into objectives considered appropriate for some pupils in infant, junior and secondary schools. The objectives selected are only some from a much wider range of possible objectives and are intended only to illustrate one way of interpreting the example aims.

It should be noted that the division between the various stages of education is an arbitrary one and it may well be that many infants could be pursuing some objectives given at the junior level, while some secondary pupils could be doing the same. Moreover, it may be considered that in some cases the progression is in steps which are too large. Again, this is because only some objectives have been selected as examples and in practice one might have many more objectives derived from any particular aim. The examples are given to illustrate the possibility of pursuing the same aims at different stages of education, thus indicating the kind of continuous development that is possible if joint planning is practised.

	AIM: to develop sympathetic attitudes towards the needs and welfare of others	AIM: to encourage pupils to make choices based on their stated values and rational judgments	AIM: to develop the ability to bring together for use information, materials and resources from a variety of sources
INFANT OBJECTIVES	1. helps others to dress after PE and at hometime	1. explains his reason for choosing a book from the reading corner	1. collects pictures of animals from magazines in order to make a book
	2. helps others with their work	2. explains why characters in a story behave as they do	2. selects materials and equipment from class shelves to paint a picture
	3. helps the teacher to give out and collect materials and equipment	3. tells the teacher why he has chosen a particular activity	3. cuts out pictures from a variety of sources to match with given word cards
	4. accepts some responsibility for the tidiness of the classroom		4. brings materials from home to help to make a model

JUNIOR OBJECTIVES			
1. offers to help teacher after school	1. chooses a holiday on the basis of stated criteria	1. locates information about raising cows in Britain to make a book
2. shows friendliness towards new pupils	2. explains the order in which he carried out a series of tasks	2. selects from general books on Norway, Egypt and the West Indies facts concerned with the weather for class presentation
3. supports school teams at weekend and after school	3. explains why ——— is his favourite book (or game, or activity, or lesson, etc.)	3. makes notes using only one side of a postcard for a 5 minute talk on how the map of Africa has changed since World War II
4. displays consideration and helpfulness towards school's domestic staff		4. selects and lists geographical facts common to countries or parts of countries which have a Mediterranean climate for an individual project

SECONDARY OBJECTIVES

1. shows concern for the welfare of others

2. displays tolerance of differences among people

3. demonstrates commitment to social improvement

4. volunteers for special social tasks to be undertaken in his own time

1. compares the prices of goods on sale

2. relates prices to other features (e.g. weight, quality, style)

3. justifies his choice of goods

1. lists and classifies sources of geographical information and the nature of that information for future use

2. compiles comparative lists of information concerning the imports and exports of Britain and Nigeria for an essay

3. selects from a variety of sources information concerning the possible effects of temperature on the design of houses for a class display

4. paraphrases information concerning the changing nature of land utilisation in agricultural areas of Britain for an individual project

5. collects information, materials and resources about the economic pros and cons of joining the Common Market with a view to a visual presentation of the results

Index